Far from Home

DATE DUE

ILL 2015			
GAYLORD			PRINTED IN U.S.A.

Far from Home

READING AND WORD STUDY

THIRD EDITION

WILLIAM P. PICKETT

THOMSON

HEINLE

Australia • Canada • Mexico • Singapore • Spain • United Kingdom • United States

THOMSON

HEINLE

Far from Home, Third Edition

William P. Pickett

Publisher, Academic ESL: *James W. Brown*
Executive Editor Dictionaries/Adult ESL: *Sherrise Roehr*
Director of Content Development: *Anita Raducanu*
Editorial Assistant: *Katherine Reilly*
Director of Product Marketing: *Amy T. Mabley*
Executive Marketing Manager: *James McDonough*
Senior Marketing Manager, Adult ESL: *Donna Lee Kennedy*

Production Editor: *Dawn Marie Elwell*
Senior Print Buyer: *Mary Beth Hennebury*
Compositor: *Interactive Composition Corporation*
Illustrator: *Katie McCormick/IllustrationOnLine.com*
Project Manager: *Neha Khattar Malhotra*
Cover/Text Designer: *Dutton and Sherman Design*
Printer: *Edwards Brothers*

Cover Image: © *Agence Images/Beateworks/Corbis*

For permission to use material from this text or product,
submit a request online at http://www.thomsonrights.com

Any additional questions about permissions can be
submitted by email to thomsonrights@thomson.com

ISBN: 1-4130-1721-5
ISBN 13: 9781413017212
(Student Edition)

ISBN: 1-4240-0445-4
ISBN 13: 9781424004454
(Audio CD)

ISBN: 1-4240-0447-0
ISBN 13: 9781424004478
(Audio Tape)

Library of Congress Control Number: 2006907369

To my son Edward

Contents

Preface

PURPOSE

Far from Home is a reader that emphasizes vocabulary development. It helps students acquire a basic vocabulary and become better readers. It accomplishes this through interesting stories and exercises that foster vocabulary development and a number of language, thinking, and study skills.

LEVEL

Far from Home is written for advanced-beginners and low-intermediate students of English as a second language. It presumes its readers know the most basic structures of English and its most common words. It presumes they know words like *wait*, *open*, *stop*, *chair*, and *beautiful*; and it teaches words like *share*, *trust*, *waste*, *struggle*, *reach*, *neighbor*, *instead*, and *however*.

CHANGES IN THE THIRD EDITION

A new section has been added to every chapter of *Far from Home*. In it, the students use the Internet to find information about a topic in the lead story. This activity is designed to give the students practice in doing searches on the Internet.

Two new stories, *A Motorcycle* and *Cholesterol*, have replaced two other stories from the second edition of *Far from Home.*

The stories, mini-dictionaries, and exercises of *Far from Home* have been modified to make them clearer and more modern. References to cell phones, e-mail, the Internet, websites, CDs, and DVDs have been included where appropriate. Some stories have been lengthened. The Creating Sentences sections have been dropped since student can do these exercises on their own.

CONTENT AND FORMAT

Lead Story and Comprehension Questions

Far from Home is divided into six units, and each unit is divided into three chapters. Every chapter begins with a picture and preview questions to stimulate students' curiosity and to activate their prior knowledge of the topics in the lead stories.

The lead stories at the beginning of each chapter describe the hopes and fears, the problems and progress of individuals and couples with roots in a variety of cultures and countries. The three lead stories in each unit are about the same person or couple.

The lead stories are followed by **Comprehension Questions**, some of which go beyond the facts of the story and require the reader to infer and make judgments.

Guessing from Context and Mini-Dictionaries

The **Guessing from Context** section precedes the **Mini-Dictionary** section. It gives the students practice in guessing the meaning of a word from the context of the sentence and the story it is in. This helps the students develop a very important skill—guessing the meaning of words from their context.

The **Mini-Dictionaries** provide brief, clear definitions of the eight key words in the lead story. More important, the **Mini-Dictionaries** give example sentences showing how the key words are actually used. The **Mini-Dictionaries** are followed by sentence-completion exercises that test, reinforce, and increase a reader's knowledge of the key words.

Story Completion and Sharing Information

Story Completion includes preview questions and a story that the reader must complete with the key words. After this cloze exercises comes **Sharing Information**, in which the key words serve as a springboard for discussion. This section gives the readers an opportunity to express their ideas and feelings and to improve their oral skills.

Word Families and Building Words with Prefixes and Suffixes

The **Word Families** section presents the more common words that are derived from the key words, or in a few cases, the words from which the key words have been derived. Finally, a **Building Words** section explains a common prefix or suffix and lists some words created by attaching this prefix or suffix. The section ends with a sentence-completion exercise using words with the prefix or suffix taught.

Using the Internet to Find Information

In this new section of *Far from Home,* students are given keywords (research topics) which they enter in the search box of a general search engine, such as Google or Yahoo. Directions lead the students to a website, and they read a page or two of the site. The students are then given the option of writing down two or three things they learned from the website.

Review Exercises

At the end of each unit are vocabulary exercises that review and reinforce the 24 key words of the unit. In addition, many of the words taught in earlier lessons are recycled in the stories and exercises of subsequent lessons.

Additional Material

A map-reading exercise or exercises in reading car ads, help-wanted ads, and real estate ads are included just before the review exercises of Units I, II, III, and IV. This content-based material relates directly to a theme of the unit and the problems of the people in it.

WORD SELECTION

The key words chosen for intensive study in **Far from Home** are high-frequency words or high-frequency idioms. Their frequency was checked with the following books: *The Teacher's Word Book of 30,000 Words* by Thorndike and Lorge; *A General Service List of English Words* by Michael West; *The American Heritage Word Frequency Book* by Carroll, Davies, and Richmann; and *3,000 Instant Words* by Sakiey and Fry.

Pronunciation Key

To show the pronunciation of a word, most English dictionaries use symbols that are as close as possible to English spelling. The **Mini-Dictionary** section of *Far from Home* also uses these symbols. They are listed below with example words that have the sound the symbols represent.

The best way to learn to pronounce words is to listen to the pronunciation of native speakers and imitate them. The **Mini-Dictionary** provides pronunciation symbols because students frequently do not have the help of native speakers.

Vowel Sounds

a	at, bad	short *a*		oo	book, good	
ā	āge, lāte	long *a*		o͞o	to͞o, fo͞od	
â(r)	câre, bâre			u	up, bus	short *u*
ä	äre, fäther			ū*	ūse, mūsic	long *u*
e	egg, bed	short *e*		û(r)	tûrn, hûrt	
ē	ēven, wē	long *e*		oi	voice, noise	
i	it, sick	short *i*		ou	out, house	
ī	īce, līfe	long *i*				
o	on, hot	short *o*				
ō	ōpen, gō	long *o*				
ô	ôff, dôg					

ə   about (ə·bout′)

elephant (el′ə·fənt)

positive (poz′ə·tiv)

today (tə·dā′)

industry (in′dəs·trē)

ə is a special symbol that indicates a reduced *a, e, i, o,* or *u.* English frequently reduces vowel sounds that are not stressed. A reduced vowel sound is called a **schwa.**

*yo͞o is also a symbol for long *u.*

Consonant Sounds

b	box, cab		p	pay, stop
ch	child, watch		r	run, dear
d	day, sad		s	sit, this
f	five, self		sh	shut, brush
g	give, bag		t	ten, but
h	hat		th	thin, teeth
j	job		*th*	*th*e, clo*th*e
k	kiss, week		v	vote, have
l	let, bill		w	want, grow
m	man, room		y	yes
n	not, sun		z	zone, buzz
ng	sing		zh	vision, garage

A Young Woman

CHAPTER 1

Far from Home

PREVIEW QUESTIONS

Discuss or think about these questions before reading the story.

1. Where is San Diego? Where is Boston? How far is it from San Diego to Boston?

2. Sometimes an unmarried son or daughter has to leave home to take a job. How do parents usually feel about this?

3. Why is moving away from home to take a job often good for a young man or woman?

Far from Home

Tomiko is an accountant and works for a large insurance company in Boston. She's the youngest of three children and has two older brothers. Tomiko was born and lived in San Diego, California, which is **far** from Boston. Her parents are from Japan.

This is Tomiko's first job, and she phones her parents every Sunday and often e-mails them. She **misses** them and they miss her. She's their "baby" and they think she's **too** young to live alone, but she laughs at that idea. She's 23 and graduated from college last year. She tells them she's happy and everything will be fine.

Tomiko **has to** be at work by 8:00. She goes to work by bus because she doesn't like to drive in Boston traffic, and it's too far to walk. After Tomiko leaves her apartment, she **hurries** to the corner to get the bus. If she misses it, she has to wait 20 minutes for the next one and gets to work late.

Tomiko is a good worker, and her employers are happy that they hired her. She spends most of her time working at her computer. She knows almost all there is to know about computers. That's why the other workers come to her for help when they have a computer problem.

Tomiko's serious about her job and never **wastes** time. At 12:00 she eats a **quick** lunch and is back at her desk by 12:30. She stops work at 4:00. She's tired by then and is happy to go home and relax.

She gets home **around** 5:00, changes her clothes, reads her e-mail, and listens to music. "I like all kinds of music," she says, "but country music is my favorite." At 5:30 she cooks dinner. She doesn't like to cook, but she has to since she lives alone and doesn't want to eat out. She usually watches the six o'clock news as she eats dinner.

COMPREHENSION QUESTIONS

Answer these questions about the story. *Use your experience and own ideas to answer questions with an asterisk (*). Work in pairs or small groups. The numbers in parentheses tell you which paragraph has the answer.*

1. Where was Tomiko born? (1)
2. What country are her parents from? (1)
*3. Do you think Tomiko can speak Japanese?
*4. She's 23. Why do her parents call her their "baby"?
5. How do her parents feel about her living alone? (2)
6. Why does she go to work by bus? (3)
7. What happens if she misses her bus? (3)
*8. Why does she have to be careful not to be late for work?
9. How does she spend most of her time at work? (4)
10. How much time does she take for lunch? (5)
11. What does she do when she gets home? (6)
12. What kind of music does she like the most? (6)

GUESSING FROM CONTEXT

Guess the meaning of the key words in these sentences. *Use the context of the story to help you. Circle your answers.*

1. Tomiko was born and lived in San Diego, California, which is **far** from Boston.

   a. bigger than
   b. very different from
   c. warmer than
   d. a great distance from

2. Tomiko is serious about her job and never **wastes** time.

   a. looks at her watch
   b. uses time poorly
   c. helps others
   d. works slowly

3. At 12:00 Tomiko eats a **quick** lunch and is back at her desk by 12:30.

   a. big
   b. hot
   c. fast
   d. small

WORD ENTRIES

> **far** / fär / *adverb:* at or to a great distance: *Tokyo is **far** from New York City.* —*adjective:* distant: *Carmen is swimming to the **far** side of the river.*
>
> **miss** / mis / *verb* **1**: not to hit, catch, or meet something or someone; not to be present: *Frank doesn't want to **miss** the dance, but he's working tonight.* **2**: to feel bad because a person or thing you love is not present: *My wife is in the hospital. The children and I **miss** her.*
>
> **too** / to͞o / *adverb:* more than is good or necessary*: *This shirt is too small. I need a bigger one.*
> *Another common meaning of **too** is *also*: *Gary is going to the park, and I want to go, **too**.*
>
> **have to** / hav to͞o *or* haf'tə / **has to** / haz to͞o *or* has'tə / *idiom:* to be necessary; must: *I **have to** clean my room. It's dirty. Carlos has a big test tomorrow. He **has to** study.*

COMPLETING SENTENCES

Complete the sentences with these words. *Use each word twice. Where a word has different endings, both forms are given.*

far	misses/missed	too	have to/has to

1. Mark can't do the math problems. They're _____ hard for him.

2. Juan came to the United States last month. He _____ his country and friends.

3. Paula _____ take the baby to the doctor for a checkup.

4. Do we have _____ to go before we get to our motel? I'm tired.

5. I'm not going to buy these shoes. They cost _____ much.

6. You can drive to the beach in five minutes. It's not _____.

7. Monica _____ class yesterday. She was sick.

8. I'm going to get home very late. I _____ phone my wife.

WORD ENTRIES

> **hur·ry** / hûr′ē / *verb:* to move fast: *Don is 80 and likes to work slowly. He doesn't like to **hurry**.* —*noun:* the act of moving fast: *Jennifer called the police and they came in a **hurry**.*
>
> **waste** / wāst / *verb:* to use something poorly; not to use: *I don't like to **waste** food. I eat everything on my plate.* —*noun:* a poor use of something: *We don't learn anything in that class. It's a **waste** of time.*
>
> **quick** / kwik / *adjective:* fast: *The problem is serious. We must take **quick** action.*
>
> **a·round** / ə-round′ / *preposition:* about; near in number or time*: *There were **around** 40 people at the party.*
> *Around has other meanings. For example, it means *on all sides of: They put a fence **around** their yard.*

COMPLETING SENTENCES

Complete the sentences with these words. *Use each word twice. Where a word has different endings, both forms are given.*

around	hurry/hurrying	quick	wasting/wasted

1. Hakeem _____ an hour waiting in line for tickets to the concert. There were none left.

2. It's _____ five miles from Cindy's house to the ocean.

3. Do we have time for a _____ drink?

4. Brian is _____ to the meeting. He doesn't want to be late.

5. The book is _____ 400 pages long.

6. No one is using those lights. Turn them off. We're _____ energy.

7. What's your _____ ? It's 6:30 and the play doesn't begin until 8:00.

8. I'm going to take a _____ shower before we eat.

Discuss or think about these questions before completing the story that follows.

1. Why is candy bad for our teeth?
2. Why is it important to floss* our teeth?
3. How often should a person go to the dentist for a checkup? Why?

   *To **floss** is *to clean between one's teeth with a thin thread.*

Complete the story with these words.

has to	waste	too	around
missed	far	quick	hurry

A Bad Toothache

Megan brushes her teeth twice a day and flosses them at night, but she has many problems with them. The difficulty is that she eats _____ much candy and doesn't go to the dentist for regular checkups.

She _____ work today because she has a bad toothache. She is going to the dentist this afternoon.

It's _____ 12:40 now, and Megan is eating a _____ lunch. She _____ be at the dentist's office by 1:00. It's not _____ to the dentist's office, but she'll have to _____ to get there on time. She doesn't have a minute to _____.

Discuss these questions and topics in pairs or small groups.

1. Do you live **far** from your parents? Where do they live?
2. Where were you born? Where did you grow up? If you moved from there, who do you **miss**? What do you miss?
3. Complete one of the following sentences. I _____ **too** much. I _____ **too** much _____.
4. Name something that you **have to** do today or tomorrow.
5. Many visitors from other countries think that people in the United States are always **hurrying**. What do you think?

6. Give some examples of how people **waste** time, food, money, and energy.

7. Some people work **quickly;** others work slowly. They take their time. Do you like to work quickly, or do you like to take your time?

8. Complete the following sentences. I usually eat dinner **around** _____. A new shirt costs **around** _____.

WORD FAMILIES

Complete the sentences with these words. *If necessary, add an ending to the word so it forms a correct sentence.* (adj. = adjective and adv. = adverb)

1. **to miss** (verb)   **missing** (adj.)

   A. I looked everywhere for the _____ check.

   B. Dan was in Europe for a week and we _____ him.

2. **quick** (adj.)   **quickly** (adv.)

   A. The ambulance came _____.

   B. Fernando took a _____ look at the menu and ordered a hamburger.

BUILDING ADVERBS WITH *-LY*

An adjective is a word that goes with a noun and tells us something about it. "It's a **clear** day." An adverb is a word that goes with a verb or adjective. "Matthew writes **clearly**." The ending, or suffix, *-ly* is added to many adjectives to form an adverb. For example, *clear + ly = clearly; quick + ly = quickly.*

When *-ly* is added to an adjective, it usually means *in a certain way.* For example, *clearly* means *in a clear way; quickly* means *in a quick way.*

Adjective	Adverb	Adjective	Adverb
careful	carefully	quick	quickly
clear	clearly	safe	safely
easy	easily	slow	slowly
free	freely	soft	softly
glad	gladly	strong	strongly
happy	happily	usual	usually
nice	nicely	warm	warmly
poor	poorly		

Use the adjectives and adverbs in parentheses to complete these sentences.

1. It was _____ to fix the TV. I fixed it _____. (easy/easily)

2. Nancy thinks _____. She's a _____ thinker. (quick/quickly)

3. The children are _____. Look how _____ they are playing. (nice/nicely)

4. Joshua is a _____ driver. He drives _____. (careful/carefully)

5. It's cold outside! Dress _____! Your _____ coat is in the closet. (warm/warmly)

6. Jackie has a _____ voice. She speaks _____. (soft/softly)

7. Jim and Beth are _____ married. They have a _____ marriage. (happy/happily)

8. Stan is a _____ worker. He works _____. (slow/slowly)

USING THE INTERNET TO FIND INFORMATION

1. *Enter* the keywords ***accountants, U.S. Department of Labor*** *in the search box of any general search engine such as Google or Yahoo. Click on the "search" button or hit "enter" on the keyboard. The search engine will lead you to a list of Web sites.*

   Click on the links to two or three of these Web sites. Look over these sites and choose the one that seems the most interesting and that tells you the most about accountants. Read a page or two. (Option: write down two or three things you learned about accountants from this site.)

2. *Enter* the keywords ***population and history of San Diego, California*** *in the search box of any general search engine such as Google or Yahoo. Click on the "search" button or hit "enter" on the keyboard. The search engine will lead you to a list of Web sites.*

   Click on the links to two or three of these Web sites. Look over these sites and choose the one that seems the most interesting and that tells you the most about San Diego. Read a page or two. (Option: write down two or three things you learned about San Diego from this site.)

CHAPTER 2

A Dog and a Boyfriend

PREVIEW QUESTIONS

Discuss or think about these questions before reading the story.

1. What are some of the problems of living alone in a big city like Boston?

2. Do you think that there is more stealing today than in the past? If so, why?

3. Why do people have dogs?

A Dog and a Boyfriend

Tomiko likes Boston. There are many interesting places to go and **a lot of** things to do, but it's not easy to live alone in a big city far from home. Tomiko never tells her parents, but sometimes she gets homesick,[1] and she often feels **afraid** at night. That's why she has three locks on her apartment door and **owns** a large dog.

The dog is a German shepherd named King. He's good company and he **protects** Tomiko. He also protects her apartment when she's at work. King is friendly if he knows you. **However**, he barks[2] at people he doesn't know. Most people are afraid of King when they hear him bark and see how big he is.

Tomiko has a boyfriend named Ted. He works in the same company as Tomiko, and he's also an accountant. He's very nice, but there's one problem. He's afraid of dogs.

The other night Ted came to visit Tomiko. She said to him, "Don't be afraid of King. He won't **bite**." But Ted doesn't **trust** King. He's too big and barks too much. Ted is afraid King **may** bite him.

Ted takes Tomiko out to dinner every Saturday night. Her favorite restaurant is Anthony's Pier 4, which has excellent fish and a great view of Boston Harbor. After dinner, they go dancing. Tomiko loves to dance and she's a very good dancer. Ted likes to dance, too, but he's not as good as Tomiko.

Tomiko and Ted also like to play tennis, and they often play on Sunday afternoon. Tomiko is a better player than Ted, but he doesn't care about winning. He's happy just to be with Tomiko.

Ted is crazy about[3] Tomiko and wants to marry her. But he knows it's too soon to ask. She likes him **a lot** and her love for him is growing, but she isn't thinking of marrying him. However, someday she may. He's the nicest boyfriend she's ever had.

---

[1] **To be homesick** is *to feel sad (or "sick") because you are away from home.*

[2] **A bark** is *the sound a dog makes.* **To bark** is *to make this sound.*

[3] **To be crazy about** is *to love very much.*

TRUE OR FALSE

If the sentence is true, write *T*. If it's false, write *F*.

_____ 1. Tomiko tells her parents that she's homesick.

_____ 2. It would be difficult to break into her apartment.

_____ 3. Most people trust King.

_____ 4. Ted works in the same company as Tomiko.

_____ 5. He's afraid King may bite him.

_____ 6. He's a better dancer than Tomiko.

_____ 7. He loves Tomiko so much he wants to marry her.

_____ 8. She wants to marry him.

WHAT DO YOU THINK?

Use your experience, ideas, and the story to answer these questions. *The story alone won't answer them.*

1. Do you think Tomiko goes out alone at night? Explain your answer.

2. Does King know that Ted is afraid of him? Explain your answer.

3. Tomiko and Ted are accountants. They like to eat out, dance, and play tennis. They have common interests. How important are common interests in making and keeping friendships?

4. Do you think Ted will marry Tomiko? Explain your answer.

Guess the meaning of the key words in these sentences. *Use the context of the story to help you. Circle your answers.*

1. There are many interesting places to go and **a lot of** things to do.

   a. educational   c. interesting
   b. many   d. great

2. King is good company and he **protects** Tomiko.

   a. loves   c. defends
   b. plays with   d. understands

3. King is friendly if he knows you. **However,** he barks at people he doesn't know.

   a. sometimes   c. now
   b. so   d. but

WORD ENTRIES

> **a lot of, a lot** / ə lot əv *or* ə-lot′ə / *idiom* **1:** a large amount or number: *Louise has **a lot of** money in the bank. She's rich.* **2:** much: *Roy studies **a lot** and does well in school.*
>
> **a·fraid** / of / ə-frād′ / *adjective:* feeling fear; nervous: *Chris is **afraid** of his boss.*
>
> **own** / ōn / *verb:* to have; to possess: *Gloria and Manuel **own** a beautiful home.* —*adjective:* belonging to oneself: *Anne has her **own** business.*
>
> **pro·tect** / prə-tekt′ / *verb:* to defend: *In the summer, I wear sunglasses to **protect** my eyes.*

COMPLETING SENTENCES

Complete the sentences with these words. *Use each word twice. Where a word has different endings, both forms are given.*

own/owns	protect/protects	afraid	a lot of/a lot

1. The little boy is _____ of the dark.

2. Alan lives in the country and _____ a large farm.

3. The Secret Service _____ the president at all times.

4. Brett drinks _____ water in the summer.

5. My daughter is 17 and has her _____ cell phone.

6. When Joy comes home late at night, she's _____.

7. Ken knows _____ about the city; he's a taxi driver.

8. Regina is careful to lock the doors at night to _____ herself and her family.

WORD ENTRIES

how·ev·er / hou·ev'ər / *conjunction:* but*: *Nicole drives very fast.* **However,** *she's never had an accident.*
*But and **however** are close in meaning. **But** is used more often than **however,** especially in conversation. **However** is more formal than **but.**

bite / bīt / *verb*:* to put one's teeth into: *Vicky is **biting** an apple.* —*noun:* *Min Ho took a **bite** of the sandwich, but he didn't like it.*
*The past tense of **bite** is **bit.**

trust / trust / *verb:* to feel that a person is honest and wants to help, or that a thing works well: *I **trust** Dave. He's nice and likes to help people.* —*noun:* a feeling that a person is honest and wants to help, or that a thing works well: *Arlene is a good friend of mine. There's a lot of **trust** between us.*

may / mā / *verb:* to be possible; to be uncertain*: *We **may** go to the movies tonight. We're not sure yet.*
***May** is also used to ask for permission to do something: ***May** I use your phone, please?*

COMPLETING SENTENCES

Complete the sentences with these words. *Use each word twice. Where a word has different endings, both forms are given.*

however	bite/bites	trust/trusts	may

1. My sister and brother-in-law _____ come to see us Sunday afternoon.

2. The bicycle cost a lot; _____, I bought it.

3. When the baby gets angry, he _____.

4. I travel a lot. I need a car I can _____.

5. Eddie and Timmy have a bad habit. They _____ their fingernails.

6. Our refrigerator is 18 years old. We _____ need a new one soon.

7. Diane has known me for many years. She _____ me.

8. The sky is clear now. _____, it's going to rain tomorrow.

Discuss or think about these questions before completing the story that follows.

1. Why do we say that a dog is man's best friend?

2. We also say that a barking dog doesn't bite. Do you think that's true?

3. What does the sign "Beware of the Dog" mean?

Complete the story with these words.

bites	however	a lot	afraid	may
a lot of	protects	own	trusts	

A Barking Dog

They say that a dog is man's best friend, and I believe that because I _____ a dog and she's very friendly. I love her _____. Her name is Sandy. She's intelligent and she can do _____ things.

They also say that a barking dog doesn't bite. You _____ believe that, too, but I don't. The dog who lives across the street from me barks at everyone, but he also _____. No one _____ him. _____, the dog's owner is happy that everyone is _____ of his dog. He's rich, and the dog _____ him and his house. In front of his house, he has a sign that says, "Beware of the Dog."

Discuss these questions and topics in pairs or small groups.

1. Complete these sentences. I eat **a lot of** _____. I _____ **a lot**.

2. Are you **afraid** of dogs? Mice? Snakes? Any other animals? If so, which ones?

3. Complete this sentence. I don't have a _____, but I would like to **own** one.

4. Some people have dogs to **protect** themselves and their homes. What other things do people use to protect themselves and their homes?

5. Complete the following sentence. There are many good things about living in the United States. **However,** _____.

6. Some dogs **bite**. What other animals will bite people? What insect often bites?

7. In general, how much do you **trust** doctors, lawyers, teachers, police officers? Give them a number between one and ten. If you have complete trust, give them a "ten." If you have no trust, give them a "one."

8. Complete this sentence. Tomorrow I **may** _____, but I'm not sure.

WORD FAMILIES

Complete the sentences with these words. *If necessary, add an ending to the word so it forms a correct sentence.* (adj. = adjective and adv. = adverb)

1. **to own** (verb)   **owner** (noun)

   A. Where is the _____ of this car? It has to be moved.

   B. Ray is a pilot and _____ a small plane.

2. **to protect** (verb)   **protection** (noun)

   protective (adj.)   **protector** (noun)

   A. Parts of the city need more police _____.

   B. When I was a little child, my older brother was my _____.

   C. Put on these gloves. They'll _____ your hands.

   D. Some parents are too _____ of their children.

3. **to trust** (verb)   **trusting** (adj.)

   A. "In God we _____" is printed on all U.S. coins and bills.

   B. Jenny believes everything she reads. She's too _____.

BUILDING NOUNS WITH -ER (-OR)

The suffix **-er** (sometimes **-or**) is added to many verbs to form a noun. For example, *teach + er = teacher; act + or = actor; wash + er = washer.*

When **-er** (or **-or**) is added to a verb, it means a person or thing that does something. For example, a *teacher* is *a person who teaches;* an *actor* is *a person who acts;* a *washer* is *a machine that washes.*

Verb	Noun	Verb	Noun
act	actor	paint	painter
dance	dancer	play	player
direct	director	sing	singer
drive	driver	teach	teacher
dry	dryer	work	worker
freeze	freezer	wash	washer
lead	leader	write	writer
own	owner		

Add -er, -or, or -r to the following verbs. Then use the nouns you form to complete the sentences. *Add an s to the nouns if necessary.*

dry	sing	write	freeze	teach	wash

1. Our history _____ is giving a test today.

2. I like O. Henry's short stories. He was a good _____.

3. Take the clothes out of the _____ and put them in the _____.

4. There's some ice cream in the _____.

5. Sylvia has a nice voice, but she's not a great _____.

own	play	lead	act	drive

6. Abraham Lincoln was a great _____.

7. Emily is taking us to the airport. I hope that she's a good _____.

8. Joe DiMaggio was a famous baseball _____.

9. The _____ are getting ready for the play.

10. I like that house, and I hear that the _____ wants to sell it.

USING THE INTERNET TO FIND INFORMATION

1. *Enter the keyword **German shepherds** in the search box of any general search engine such as Google or Yahoo. Click on the "search" button or hit "enter" on the keyboard. The search engine will lead you to a list of Web sites.*

   Click on the links to two or three of these Web sites. Look over these sites and choose the one that seems the most interesting and that tells you the most about German shepherds. Read a page or two. (Option: write down two or three things you learned about German shepherds from this site.)

2. *Enter the keywords **population and history of Boston, Massachusetts** in the search box of any general search engine such as Google or Yahoo. Click on the "search" button or hit "enter" on the keyboard. The search engine will lead you to a list of Web sites.*

   Click on the links to two or three of these Web sites. Look over these sites and choose the one that seems the most interesting and that tells you the most about Boston. Read a page or two. (Option: write down two or three things you learned about Boston from this site.)

CHAPTER 3

Fish for Dinner

PREVIEW QUESTIONS

Discuss or think about these questions before reading the story.

1. Do you want to lose weight, gain weight, or stay the same?

2. Why do people try to lose weight? Give at least two reasons.

3. Many people in the United States go on diets to lose weight. Are diets common in other countries? If not, why not?

Fish for Dinner

Tomiko is short and a little heavy. She's **only** five feet two inches tall, and she **weighs** 125 pounds. That's not bad; the problem is that she's gaining **weight.** When she came to Boston, she weighed only 110 pounds. She knows she'll feel and look better if she **loses** a little weight.

Three other people in Tomiko's office are also on a diet, but that's not surprising. In the United States, it seems that everyone is on a diet or thinking about one. Go to any bookstore and you'll see many diet books, and all of them will show you a different way to lose weight.

Tomiko started her diet yesterday morning. "I want to lose ten pounds," she says, "but I'm not in a hurry. I know that most people who lose weight quickly gain it back. My friend went on a diet and lost 15 pounds in a month. Three months later, she weighed more than when she started her diet."

Although Tomiko is **trying** to lose only a pound or two a week, it's hard. The problem is that she loves to eat. She especially loves ice cream and chocolate candy, but she can't have them on her diet.

Tomiko isn't on a special diet like Weight Watchers. She's on her own diet. She's not eating any bread, butter, dessert, or candy. And she's trying to eat a little less of everything.

Tomiko has been very good today. She had orange juice, cereal, and a cup of coffee with a little milk for breakfast. For lunch, she had a lettuce and tomato salad and soup. She hasn't had anything between meals.

It's **almost** 6:00 now and Tomiko is **starving**. She's having fish, carrots, and broccoli for dinner. She **enjoys** fish and most vegetables. That's great because fish and vegetables are good for you, and they don't have many calories.[1]

---

[1] A **calorie** tells *how much heat or energy a food has.* An apple has about 80 **calories**.

Answer these questions about the story. *Use your experience and own ideas to answer questions with an asterisk (*). Work in pairs or small groups. The numbers in parentheses tell you which paragraph has the answer.*

 1. How tall is Tomiko? (1)

 2. How much does she weigh? (1)

 *3. Why do you think she gained weight when she came to Boston?

 4. What does it seem that everyone in the United States is doing or thinking about? (2)

 5. How many pounds does Tomiko want to lose? (3)

 6. Why isn't she in a hurry to lose weight? (3)

 *7. Why is it bad to lose weight too quickly?

 8. Why is it hard for Tomiko to lose weight? (4)

 9. What isn't she eating? Name four things. (5)

 10. What did she have for breakfast? (6)

 11. What is she having for dinner? (7)

 *12. Do you think she will lose ten pounds? Explain your answer.

GUESSING FROM CONTEXT

Guess the meaning of the key words in these sentences. *Use the context of the story to help you. Circle your answers.*

 1. Tomiko *is **trying** to lose* only a pound or two a week.

    a. is not able to lose   c. is doing what she can to lose

    b. is thinking about losing   d. doesn't want to lose

 2. It's almost 6:00 now and Tomiko is **starving.**

    a. cooking   c. resting

    b. happy   d. very hungry

 3. Tomiko **enjoys** fish and most vegetables. That's great because fish and vegetables are good for you.

    a. eats   c. doesn't like

    b. likes   d. buys

WORD ENTRIES

> **on·ly** / ōn'lē / *adverb:* and no more; and no other: *I have **only** $100 in the bank.*
> —*adjective:* and nothing else; and no one else; *Paul was the **only** student who didn't pass the test.*
>
> **weigh** / wā / *verb:* to have a weight of; to be a certain weight: *The small bags of potatoes **weigh** five pounds.*
>
> **weight** / wāt / *noun:* how heavy a person or thing is: *The baby is getting big. What's his **weight**?*
>
> **lose** / lōōz / *verb** **1:** to have something and then not be able to find it: *I don't know where my ring is. I hope I didn't **lose** it.* **2:** to have less of something: *Gabe is **losing** his hair. He's not so young anymore.* **3:** to fail to win; to be defeated: *Our football team **lost** last Saturday. The other team was bigger and better.*
> **The past tense of **lose** is **lost**.*
>
> **al·though** / ôl-thō' / *conjunction:* in contrast to the fact that*: ***Although** I slept well last night, I feel tired.*
> ****Though** has the same meaning and is used in the same way as **although**.*

COMPLETING SENTENCES

Complete the sentences with these words. *Use each word twice. Where a word has different endings, both forms are given.*

losing/lost	only	weigh/weight	although

1. The radio is _____ $20. I'm going to buy it.

2. _____ it's raining, I'm going for a walk.

3. Leslie _____ her keys and can't find them.

4. Kevin looks thin. How much does he _____?

5. Glen smokes _____ he knows he shouldn't.

6. Audrey has a _____ problem. She's over 200 pounds.

7. The basketball is soft. It's _____ air.

8. _____ Donna knows where the money is.

MINI-DICTIONARY—PART TWO

WORD ENTRIES

> **try** / trī / *verb:* to do what one can; to make an effort: *Carlos is* **trying** *to learn English quickly.* —*noun: Joan didn't catch the ball, but she made a nice* **try**.
>
> **al·most** / ôl′mōst *or* ôl-mōst′ / *adverb:* a little less than; close to: *It's* **almost** *a mile to the supermarket.*
>
> **starve** / stärv / *verb* **1:** to be very hungry: *Sandra didn't eat breakfast. She must be* **starving**. **2:** to die because one has no food: *In the winter, some animals* **starve** *because they can't find food.*
>
> **en·joy** / in-joi′ / *verb:* to like; to get pleasure from: *Dick* **enjoys** *playing cards with his friends.*

COMPLETING SENTENCES

Complete the sentences with these words. *Use each word twice. Where a word has different endings, both forms are given.*

enjoy/enjoyed	try/trying	almost	starve/starving

1. Let's eat now. I'm _____.

2. Brenda is _____ to find a better job. She wants to make more money.

3. I _____ cut myself with that knife.

4. We _____ the movie. It was interesting.

5. Are the children _____ ready to go to school?

6. We always feed the birds when it snows. We don't want them to _____.

7. _____ yourself at the party!

8. I may not be able to climb to the top of the mountain, but I'm going to _____.

Discuss or think about these questions before completing the story that follows.

1. Name some foods that have a lot of calories.

2. Name some foods low in calories.

3. Why are some people thin although they eat a lot?

Complete the story with these words.

lose	almost	trying	weight	starving
although	only	weighs	enjoys	

Very Different Problems

My friend Rafael _____ 105 pounds _____ he eats a lot and _____ big meals. He's _____ to gain 15 pounds, but up to now he's been able to gain _____ one.

I have a very different problem. I'm 220 pounds and want to _____ 30. That's why I'm on a diet, but so far my _____ hasn't changed.

It's _____ time for lunch, and Rafael and I are _____. We're going to a diner. I'm having a small tuna fish salad and a diet Coke. He's getting a large cheeseburger, french fries, and apple pie with vanilla ice cream.

Discuss these questions and topics in pairs or small groups.

1. When a family has **only** one child, we say that boy or girl is an only child. Are you an only child? If not, how many brothers do you have? And sisters?

2. Some people go on a diet, lose a lot of **weight**, and then gain it all back. Do you know anyone who did this? Did you ever do it?

3. Did you ever **lose** anything that was valuable, such as a ring, watch, money, or important papers? If so, how did it happen? Did you find it (or them) again?

4. Complete this sentence. **Although** I don't like to _____, I have to.

5. Think about what you do, and complete this sentence. I'm **trying** to

   _____.

6. Tell your classmates about something that **almost** happened to you, such as an accident. Or tell about something you almost did.

7. **Starve** usually means *to be very hungry,* but it also means *to die because there is nothing to eat.* Is there any part of the world where people still starve? If so, where? Why is there little or no food there?

8. Name some activities that you **enjoy**.

WORD FAMILIES

Complete the sentences with these words. *If necessary, add an ending to the word so it forms a correct sentence.* (adj. = adjective and adv. = adverb)

1. **to lose** (verb)   **loser** (noun)   **loss** (noun)   **lost** (adj.)

   A. When I play tennis, I try hard to win, but I also know how to be a good

      _____.

   B. Jessica is upset about the _____ of her watch.

   C. As soon as I get my paycheck, I put it in my wallet. I don't want to

      _____ it.

   D. We're looking for a _____ dog. I hope we find him soon.

2. **to starve** (verb)   **starvation** (noun)

   A. In the winter of 1620–1621, the Pilgrims who came to Plymouth, Massachusetts, faced _____.

   B. When my son comes home from school, he goes to the kitchen to get something to eat. He's _____.

3. **to enjoy** (verb)   **enjoyment** (noun)   **enjoyable** (adj.)

   A. Linda gets a lot of _____ from playing the piano.

   B. I hope you _____ the play.

   C. Our trip to Florida was _____.

BUILDING NOUNS WITH -*MENT*

The suffix -**ment** is added to verbs to form a noun. For example, *pay + ment = payment;*
command + ment = commandment.

When -**ment** is added to a verb, it usually means *the act of* or *the result of.* For
example, *a payment* is *the act of* or *the result of paying; a commandment* is *the result of
giving a command.*

Verb	Noun	Verb	Noun
advance	advancement	govern	government
announce	announcement	judge	judgment
appoint	appointment	move	movement
arrange	arrangement	pay	payment
command	commandment	place	placement
employ	employment	state	statement
enjoy	enjoyment		

Circle the letter next to the word that best completes the sentence.

1. I have one more _____ to make on my new car.

   a. statement   c. payment
   b. movement   d. placement

2. The _____ for our trip to Hawaii are complete.

   a. advancements   c. announcements
   b. arrangements   d. judgments

3. Riding her new bicycle is giving Gina a lot of _____.

   a. employment   c. movement
   b. advancement   d. enjoyment

4. The president is going to make some important _____ on TV tonight.

   a. announcements   c. arrangements
   b. placements   d. judgments

5. You made a _____ about me that I don't like.

   a. commandment   c. movement
   b. appointment   d. statement

6. The United States and France have strong central _____.

    a. arrangements   c. governments

    b. placements   d. employment

7. People are living longer today because of _____ in the field of medicine.

    a. appointments   c. statements

    b. advancements   d. judgments

8. The exam helps in the _____ of the students in the right classes.

    a. placement   c. employment

    b. announcement   d. payment

USING THE INTERNET TO FIND INFORMATION

1. *Enter the keyword **diet books** in the search box of any general search engine such as Google or Yahoo. Click on the "search" button or hit "enter" on the keyboard. The search engine will lead you to a list of Web sites.*

   Click on the links to two or three of these Web sites. Look over these sites and choose the one that seems the most interesting and that tells you the most about diet books. Read a page or two. (Option: write down the names of two or three diet books you saw on this site.)

2. *Enter the keyword **Weight Watchers** in the search box of any general search engine such as Google or Yahoo. Click on the "search" button or hit "enter" on the keyboard. The search engine will lead you to a list of Web sites.*

   Click on the links to two or three of these Web sites. Look over these sites and choose the one that seems the most interesting and that tells you the most about Weight Watchers. Read a page or two. (Option: write down two or three things you learned about Weight Watchers from this site.)

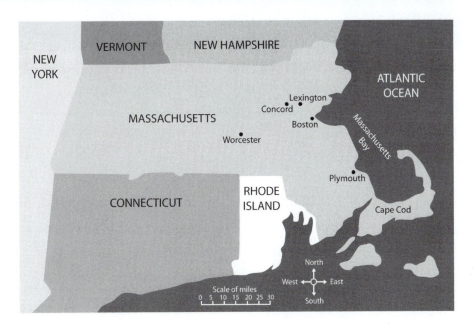

MASSACHUSETTS

Answer these questions about Massachusetts, Tomiko's new home.

1. What two states are south of Massachusetts?

2. What two states are north of Massachusetts?

3. What state is west of Massachusetts?

4. Are Lexington and Concord northeast or northwest of Boston?

5. Is Plymouth southeast or southwest of Boston?

6. What famous cape is southeast of Boston?

7. On what ocean is the coast of Massachusetts?

8. About how many miles is it from Boston to Worcester?

ACTIVITY

Bring to class a map of the state in which you live. *Work with a partner and make up ten questions about your state.*

SYNONYMS

Next to each sentence, write the word that has the same meaning or almost the same meaning as the part of the sentence in bold (dark) print.

missed	hurries	a lot of	starving
have to	almost	only	enjoys

1. _____ The southern part of the United States doesn't get **much** snow.
2. _____ It's been a long trip, but we're **close to** home now.
3. _____ Ron **wasn't at** the meeting. He didn't feel well.
4. _____ Hillary **likes** her science and history classes.
5. _____ I have a friend who never **moves fast**.
6. _____ **No one but** Sam has a key to the office.
7. _____ We **must** finish the job today.
8. _____ Is there a restaurant near here? I'm **very hungry**.

SENTENCE COMPLETION

Complete the sentences with these words.

quickly	far	may	however
trying	owns	around	waste

1. I'm going to have my eyes examined. I _____ need glasses.
2. Barbara _____ a motorboat that she uses a lot.
3. Many people _____ water because it's cheap.
4. Felix is _____ to do better in school.
5. Shawn and Terry did the dishes _____ and went to the movies.
6. My new laptop computer costs _____ $1,000.
7. How _____ is it to the post office?
8. Grace is 85; _____, she's very active.

STORY COMPLETION

Complete the story with these words.

afraid	weighs	lose	trust
protect	bite	too	although

Lions

Lions are the largest members of the cat family. An adult lion _____ 400 pounds. _____ the lion is the king of the animal world, it spends most of the day sleeping and resting.

Lions live in groups, and they attack, _____, and kill other animals. That's why no animals _____ them.

India and some countries in Africa have laws to _____ lions because people have killed _____ many of them. These countries are _____ that they will _____ all of their lions.

A Young Couple

CHAPTER 4

Sharing the Housework
page 32

CHAPTER 5

Rushing the Baby to the Hospital
page 42

CHAPTER 6

Fords, Hondas, and Toyotas
page 52

Sharing the Housework

PREVIEW QUESTIONS

Discuss or think about these questions before reading the story.

1. Why is it difficult to be a taxi driver in a large city like New York?

2. Why is it also good to be a taxi driver in a large city?

3. When a wife works full-time, does the husband usually do half of the housework? If not, why not?

Sharing the Housework

Frank and Sue are married and have two young children. Frank is a taxi driver in New York City, one of the best cities in the world to be a taxi driver in, and also one of the worst. It's one of the best because you never have to wait long for passengers, and taxis cost a lot, so you can make good money. It's one of the worst because traffic is heavy, and everyone is in a hurry.

When Frank and Sue got married, they thought she would stay home and take care of the children, and he would make the money to pay the bills. But that's not the way it is. Food, clothing, and their new house cost more than he makes. Sue has to work, too. She's a teacher's aide at P.S. 63 in Manhattan.

Since **both** of them work, Frank and Sue **share** the housework. "That's the way it should be," Sue says, "but some of my friends work full-time and their husbands don't do any housework. Frank does all the cooking, and I keep the house clean and wash the clothes."

Frank had never cooked in his life. The first night he tried, he **burned** the rice, and the chicken didn't taste right. Frank and Sue **still** laugh about his first dinner. He'll never be a great cook, but he's **improving** fast. He likes to cook spaghetti and meatballs, and they taste very good. Learning to cook was difficult for Frank, but now he thinks cooking is **fun**.

When Frank cooks, Sue washes the dishes and he **wipes** them dry. Although he likes to cook, he **hates** to do the dishes. That's why he wants to buy a dishwasher. Sue also thinks it's a good idea, so they're going to buy one when they get a little extra money.

When they finish the dishes and the children are in bed, Frank and Sue read, watch TV, or talk. It's the only time during the day when they have the chance to enjoy a little peace and quiet. Their work and their children don't leave them much time for themselves.

COMPREHENSION QUESTIONS

Answer these questions about the story. *Use your experience and own ideas to answer questions with an asterisk (*). Work in pairs or small groups. The numbers in parentheses tell you which paragraph has the answer.*

1. Why is New York City one of the best places to be a taxi driver? (1)

2. Why is it one of the worst? (1)

*3. Compare driving a taxi in a small city to driving one in New York? What are some of the differences?

4. Why does Sue have to work? (2)

*5. What do teachers' aides do? How do they help teachers?

6. What happens at some of Sue's friends' homes? (3)

*7. Do you think Sue's friends are angry with their husbands because they don't help with the housework? Explain your answer.

8. What happened the first night Frank cooked? (4)

9. What does he like to cook? (4)

10. What does he hate to do? (5)

11. What do Frank and Sue want to buy? When are they going to buy one? (5)

12. When do they enjoy a little peace and quiet? (6)

GUESSING FROM CONTEXT

Guess the meaning of the key words in these sentences. *Use the context of the story to help you. Circle your answers.*

1. Since both of them work, Frank and Sue **share** the housework.

   a. don't do
   b. do later
   c. pay someone to do
   d. divide

2. Frank will never be a great cook, but he's **improving** fast.

   a. getting better
   b. changing
   c. working
   d. getting worse

3. Although Frank likes to cook, he **hates** to do the dishes.

   a. also likes to
   b. doesn't like to
   c. also has to
   d. won't

WORD ENTRIES

> **both** / bōth / *adjective:* the one and the other; the two: ***Both** dresses are pretty, but I can buy only one.* —*pronoun: Ramón and Alice are friends, and **both** are lawyers.*
>
> **share** / shâr / *verb:* to do or use with others; to divide: *Roberta bought a box of candy and **shared** it with her friends.* —*noun:* the part of something one owns, does, or uses with others: *George is lazy. He doesn't do his **share** of the work.*
>
> **burn** / bûrn / *verb* **1:** to be on fire; to destroy by heat: *The building is **burning**! Call the fire department!* **2:** to hurt by fire or heat: *The plate is hot. If you touch it, you'll **burn** your fingers.* —*noun:* injury caused by fire or heat: *Esther was in a fire. She has **burns** on her face and arms.*
>
> **still** / stil / *adverb* **1:** up to now and at this time, too*; continuing to: *It's 11:00 P.M. and Greg is **still** studying.* **2:** up to then and at that time, too: *When I left the office, the boss was **still** working.*
> ***Still** can also mean not moving: *Stop walking and listen. Be **still**.*

COMPLETING SENTENCES

Complete the sentences with these words. *Use each word twice. Where a word has different endings, both forms are given.*

share/shares	still	burn/burning	both

1. I'm pleased when my son _____ his toys with his younger brother.

2. Our basketball team won by 12 points, but _____ teams played well.

3. Is it _____ snowing?

4. Be careful with that hot iron! Don't _____ yourself!

5. Miss Martinez is a better teacher than Mrs. Allan, but _____ are very good.

6. Does your daughter _____ want to be a dentist?

7. If we win the lottery, we'll _____ the money.

8. I smell smoke. What's _____?

WORD ENTRIES

> **im·prove** / im-proov' / *verb:* to do or become better: *Chen still makes a lot of errors, but his English is **improving**.*
>
> **fun** / fun / *noun:* pleasure; a good time: *I love to dance. It's **fun**.*
>
> **wipe** / wīp / *verb:* to move a cloth over something to clean or dry it: *The waiter cleared and **wiped** the table.*
>
> **hate** / hāt / *verb:* to dislike strongly: *Our son **hates** to clean his room.* —*noun:* strong dislike: ***Hate** is the opposite of love.*

COMPLETING SENTENCES

Complete the sentences with these words. *Use each word twice. Where a word has different endings, both forms are given.*

wipe/wiping	hate/hates	fun	improves/improving

1. Have_____ at the picnic!

2. Cathy is _____ the baby's hands and face.

3. I hope the weather _____. It's raining, and I want to go for a walk this afternoon.

4. Bob loves to read, but he _____ to study for tests.

5. _____ your shoes on the mat before you go into the house. They're dirty.

6. We spent three days at Disney World, and we had a lot of _____.

7. I _____ to be late for work.

8. Pat doesn't play the guitar very well, but she's taking lessons and she's _____.

STORY COMPLETION

Discuss or think about these questions before completing the story that follows.

1. Do you spend much time in the sun in the summer?
2. Why is it bad to get too much sun?
3. What can we do to protect our skin from the sun?

Complete the story with these words.

wiped	still	improving	share
hates	both	fun	burn

Too Much Sun

Sharon and Amy graduated from college last year. _____ of them work for International Business Machines (IBM). Sharon repairs business machines, and Amy is a computer programmer. They're single and they _____ an apartment.

Sharon and Amy like to swim. Yesterday was a warm, sunny day, so they went to the beach and had a lot of _____. After Sharon went for a swim, she _____ her face and arms with a towel and laid in the sun. She wished she hadn't. She got a very bad _____, and it _____ hurts today.

Amy thinks Sharon should see a doctor, but she _____ to go to doctors. She says she's _____ and will be fine in a few days. She thinks going to a doctor would be a waste of time and money.

SHARING INFORMATION

Discuss these questions and topics in pairs or small groups.

1. Complete the following sentence about the United States and Canada. **Both** countries _____.

2. Give an example of something you **share** with others. Why is sharing so important?

3. Did you ever **burn** yourself? How? Was the burn bad? Did you put anything on it? Did you have to see a doctor?

4. What city did you live in last year? Do you **still** live in the same city?

5. Why are you studying English? Give two or three reasons. Is your English **improving**? What are you doing to improve it?

6. Name some things that are **fun** to do.

7. All cars, buses, and trucks have **wipers**. Where are the wipers, and what do they do?

8. Name some things that you **hate** to do.

WORD FAMILIES

Complete the sentences with these words. *If necessary, add an ending to the word so it forms a correct sentence.* (adj. = adjective and adv. = adverb)

1. **to burn** (verb)　　　　　　**burner** (noun)

   A. We have a new oil _____. It's much better than our old one.

   B. Is the fire still _____?

2. **to improve** (verb)　　　　**improvement** (noun)

   A. Your schoolwork was poor last year. I want to see some _____ this year.

   B. Sal had a heart attack, but he's _____ and will leave the hospital soon.

3. **fun** (noun)   **funny*** (adj.)

   A. Marge and I go bowling every Friday night. It's _____.

   B. Everyone laughed at the clown. He was very _____.

   ***Fun** and **funny** have different meanings. **Fun** means *a good time*. **Funny** means *causing laughter or a smile*.

4. **to hate** (verb)   **hatred** (noun)

   A. Rosa is from the Dominican Republic, and she _____ cold weather.

   B. _____ can easily lead to fighting and violence.

BUILDING ADJECTIVES WITH -Y

The suffix *-y* is added to nouns to form an adjective, for example, *dirt + y = dirty*; *rain + y = rainy*.

When *-y* is added to a noun to form an adjective, it usually means *full of* or *a lot of*. For example, *dirty* means *full of* or *a lot of dirt; rainy* means *a lot of rain*.

Noun	Adjective	Noun	Adjective
dirt	dirty	rain	rainy
fun	funny	rock	rocky
health	healthy	salt	salty
ice	icy	sun	sunny
juice	juicy	thirst	thirsty
luck	lucky	wind	windy
noise	noisy		

Circle the letter next to the word that best completes the sentence.

1. I want a soda; I'm _____.

   a. healthy   c. thirsty
   b. lucky   d. dirty

2. There are no clouds in the sky. It's going to be a _____day.

   a. windy   c. healthy
   b. noisy   d. sunny

3. Our team was _____. That's why we won the game.

   a. thirsty   c. funny
   b. lucky   d. rocky

4. These clothes are _____. I have to wash them.

   a. dirty   c. juicy
   b. salty   d. rocky

5. A lot of people were at the party. It was _____.

   a. lucky   c. healthy
   b. noisy   d. windy

6. These oranges are _____.

   a. icy   c. dirty
   b. salty   d. juicy

7. Be careful! The streets and sidewalks are _____.

   a. rocky   c. icy
   b. windy   d. rainy

8. I don't like the way this food tastes. It's too _____.

   a. salty   c. dirty
   b. healthy   d. juicy

USING THE INTERNET TO FIND INFORMATION

1. *Enter the keywords **taxi drivers, U.S. Department of Labor** in the search box of any general search engine such as Google or Yahoo. Click on the "search" button or hit "enter" on the keyboard. The search engine will lead you to a list of Web sites.*

   Click on the links to two or three of these Web sites. Look over these sites and choose the one that seems the most interesting and that tells you the most about taxi drivers. Read a page or two. (Option: write down two or three things you learned about taxi drivers from this site.)

2. *Enter the keyword **sharing housework** in the search box of any general search engine such as Google or Yahoo. Click on the "search" button or hit "enter" on the keyboard. The search engine will lead you to a list of Web sites.*

   Click on the links to two or three of these Web sites. Look over these sites and choose the one that seems the most interesting and that tells you the most about sharing housework. Read a page or two. (Option: write down two or three things you learned about sharing housework from this site.)

CHAPTER 5

Rushing the Baby to the Hospital

PREVIEW QUESTIONS

Discuss or think about these questions before reading the story.

1. Why is the first grade so important in a child's education?

2. Babies love to touch things. Why is this good?

3. What things do we have to keep away from babies?

Rushing the Baby to the Hospital

Frank and Sue have a son and daughter, and they're very **proud** of them. Their son's name is Frank, and they call him Frankie. He's six years old and in the first grade. He's a good student and he enjoys school. He's learning to read and to add.

After school, Frankie plays with his friends. "Baseball is my favorite sport," he says, "and I love to play catch with my dad. In the summer he takes me to some Yankee[1] games. I'm going to play for the Yankees someday."

Their daughter is two years old, and her name is Sarah. She's beginning to talk. She's a very active baby who likes to **explore** and touch everything. That's great because that's the way a baby learns, but it's also a problem. You have to watch Sarah all the time. **Fortunately**, Sue's mom lives near Sue and Frank, and she takes care of the baby when Sue is working. It's not easy to take care of a two year old, but Grandma loves it. She thinks Sarah is the cutest baby in the world.

Frank and Sue are careful not to put medicine or cleaning materials where Sarah can get them. They keep their medicine in the bathroom cabinet. They're afraid Sarah might think it's candy and take some. And they keep cleaning materials in a cabinet over the kitchen sink.

However, last Saturday Sue left a bottle of bleach under the kitchen sink. That was a big **mistake.** Sarah was playing in the kitchen, and she **swallowed** some bleach.[2] Bleach is a **poison** and can kill a baby. Fortunately, Sue saw what happened.

Frank and Sue didn't waste a second. They **rushed** Sarah to the hospital. It's about a mile from their house. They got there in two minutes. The doctor talked to Sue because he had to know what the baby had swallowed.

The doctor examined Sarah and gave her some medicine. They kept her in the hospital for five hours and watched her. Fortunately, she swallowed only a little **bit** of bleach and was OK. When she arrived home, she got a lot of hugs and kisses from her grandmother and Frankie.

---

[1] The New York Yankees are a major league baseball team. They play in the Bronx, which is part of New York City.

[2] **Bleach** is *a liquid or powder used to make clothes brighter.*

TRUE OR FALSE

If the sentence is true, write *T*. If it's false, write *F*.

_____ 1. Frankie doesn't like school.

_____ 2. Baseball is his favorite sport.

_____ 3. It's easy to take care of Sarah.

_____ 4. Frank and Sue keep their medicine in the bathroom cabinet.

_____ 5. Sue left some bleach where Sarah could get it.

_____ 6. Frank and Sue got to the hospital quickly.

_____ 7. Sarah spent two days in the hospital.

_____ 8. She swallowed a lot of bleach.

WHAT DO YOU THINK?

Use your experience, ideas, and the story to answer these questions.

1. Frank plays with his son and takes him to baseball games. Is spending time with Frankie important? If so, why?

2. Frankie thinks he's going to play for the Yankees. Do you think his parents should let him think that? Or should they tell him it'll probably never happen? Explain your answer.

3. Grandparents are almost always easier on children than parents. For example, they punish them less. Why?

4. Do you think Frank got angry at Sue for leaving the bleach under the sink? Do you think he said anything to her? Explain your answer.

Guess the meaning of the key words in these sentences. *Use the context of the story to help you. Circle your answers.*

1. Sarah is a very active baby who likes to **explore** and touch everything.

   a. play
   b. look at things carefully

   c. laugh
   d. cry

2. Sue left a bottle of bleach under the kitchen sink. That was a big **mistake.**

   a. fear
   b. loss

   c. error
   d. improvement

3. Sarah was playing in the kitchen and **swallowed** some bleach.

   a. touched
   b. opened

   c. smelled
   d. drank

MINI-DICTIONARY—PART ONE

WORD ENTRIES

proud / proud / *adjective* **1**: very happy with what one has or does: *Joe is* **proud** *of his wife. She's smart and very nice.* **2**: having too high opinion of oneself: *Dennis thinks he's better than anyone else. He's* **proud**.

ex·plore / ək-splôr′ / *verb* **1**: to go through and look carefully at an area: *Columbus* **explored** *the Caribbean and many of its islands.* **2**: to look carefully at an idea: *Doctors are* **exploring** *new ways of treating cancer.*

for·tu·nate·ly / fôr′chə-nit-lē / *adverb*: by good luck; luckily: *Ling lost the key to her car.* **Fortunately,** *she had another one.*

mis·take / mi-stāk′ / *noun*: error: *No one is perfect. We all make* **mistakes**. —*verb*: to think that one thing or person is another: *I frequently* **mistake** *Tom for his twin brother.*

COMPLETING SENTENCES

Complete the sentences with these words. *Use each word twice. Where a word has different endings, both forms are given.*

fortunately	explore/explored	proud	mistake/mistakes

1. I don't like this book. It was a _____ to buy it.

2. Exxon Mobil _____ the area for oil, but didn't find any.

3. Kristin is _____ of her new car.

4. We went to the park for a picnic. _____, the weather was nice.

5. Psychiatrists _____ people's feelings and problems.

6. I got an A in math. I'm _____ of myself.

7. Miguel was in an auto accident. _____, he was wearing a seat belt and wasn't hurt.

8. Laura wrote an interesting composition, but she made a lot of spelling _____.

MINI-DICTIONARY—PART TWO

WORD ENTRIES

swal·low / swol′ō / *verb:* to move food or drink down one's throat: *These pills are large. It's difficult to **swallow** them.*

poi·son / poi′zən / *noun:* any substance that can kill: *Someone put **poison** in the cat's food and killed her.* —*verb:* to kill or hurt with poison: *The smoke from the factories is **poisoning** our air.*

rush / rush / *verb:* to move fast; to hurry: *The fire engines are **rushing** to the fire.* —*noun:* the act of moving fast: *Abdul can't wait for us. He's in a **rush**.*

bit / bit / *noun:* a small amount: *We need some fresh air in this room. Please open the window a **bit**.*

COMPLETING SENTENCES

Complete the sentences with these words. *Use each word twice. Where a word has different endings, both forms are given.*

rush/rushes	poison/poisoning	bit	swallow/swallowing

1. Mike is lazy. He didn't do a _____ of work today.
2. Debbie _____ home from work every afternoon.
3. I have a sore throat. It hurts to _____.
4. The soldiers were afraid that the enemy would use _____ gas.
5. Chew your food well before _____ it.
6. The ice cream tastes very good. May I have a _____ more?
7. The chemicals we're using to kill insects are _____ our water.
8. What's your _____? We're not going anywhere.

STORY COMPLETION

Discuss or think about these questions before completing the story that follows.

1. Why is it easier to care for a dog in the country than in a city?
2. Are you afraid of mice? If so, why?
3. What do people use to kill mice?

Complete the story with these words.

mistake	rushed	proud	fortunately
bit	poison	swallowed	explore

Vet* Saves Dog

Paul has a beautiful dog named Wolf and a nice house in the country. Paul and Wolf like to go for long walks and to _____ the woods near his house. Paul is _____ of his dog and house, but there's a problem with the house. When the weather turns cold, mice from the fields get into it. Paul isn't afraid of mice, but he doesn't like to have them running around his house.

Yesterday he bought some powder to _____ the mice. He put the powder in a dish next to the refrigerator, but that was a _____. Wolf thought the powder was food, and he _____ some. _____, Paul had put only a _____ of powder in the dish.

When Wolf got sick, Paul knew it was the powder, and he _____ the dog to a veterinarian.* The vet was able to save Wolf. On the way home, Paul bought some mousetraps and cheese.

_____

* A **veterinarian** is *an animal doctor* and is often called a **vet**.

SHARING INFORMATION

Discuss these questions and topics in pairs or small groups.

1. Complete the following sentence. I'm **proud** of _____
   _____.

2. What are some of the good things that have come from the **exploration** of space by the United States and other countries?

3. Complete the following sentence. I'm **fortunate** that _____
   _____.

4. Everyone makes **mistakes.** Tell your classmates about a mistake that you or another person made.

5. It's difficult to **swallow** food when your throat hurts. What kind of food do people usually eat when they have a sore throat?

6. Bleach is a **poison.** Are any other cleaning materials poisonous?

7. Eight o'clock in the morning and five o'clock at night are called "**rush** hours." Why?

8. Sometimes we use "a **bit**" followed by an adjective. For example, "I'm a bit hungry." Which of these sentences describe how you feel now?

   a. I'm not thirsty.
   b. I'm a bit thirsty.
   c. I'm very thirsty.

WORD FAMILIES

Complete the sentences with these words. *If necessary, add an ending to the word so it forms a correct sentence.* (adj. = adjective and adv. = adverb)

1. **proud** (adj.)   **proudly** (adv.)   **pride** (noun)

   A. Gladys is in the army and wears her uniform _____.

   B. Andy and Yuri are excellent carpenters. They take _____ in their work.

   C. We are _____ of our school. It's one of the best in the state.

2. **to explore** (verb)   **explorer** (noun)   **exploration** (noun)

   A. In the sixteenth century, Spain sent many _____ to North and South America.

   B. England, France, and Spain were the leaders in the _____ of North America.

   C. President Thomas Jefferson sent Lewis and Clark to _____ the Louisiana Territory, which the United States purchased from France.

3. **fortunately** (adv.)   **fortunate** (adj.)
   unfortunate (adj.)   **unfortunately** (adv.)

   A. I went to a casino in Atlantic City to try my luck. _____, I lost a lot of money.

   B. Elena never gets sick. She's _____.

   C. Someone stole my car. _____, the police found it, and I got it back.

   D. It's _____ that the factory is closing. Many people will lose their jobs.

4. **mistake** (noun)   **mistaken** (adj.)

   A. Many people come to the United States with the _____ idea that it's easy to get rich here.

   B. I put salt in the sugar bowl by _____.

5. **poison** (noun)   **poisonous** (adj.)

   A. The leaves of some plants contain _____.

   B. Some snakes are _____.

BUILDING WORDS WITH *UN-*

The prefix **un-** is placed before many adjectives, adverbs, and verbs to form a new word. When **un-** is placed before an adjective or adverb, it means *not* or *the opposite of*. For example, *un + happy = unhappy*, which means *not happy; un + fortunately = unfortunately*, which means *the opposite of fortunately*.

When **un-** is placed before a verb, it indicates an action that is the opposite of that verb. For example, *un + dress = undress; un + lock = unlock; un + cover = uncover; un + do = undo*. *Undress, unlock, uncover*, and *undo* are the opposites of *dress, lock, cover*, and *do*.

Adjective, Adverb, or Verb	New Word	Adjective, Adverb, or Verb	New Word
able	unable	healthy	unhealthy
afraid	unafraid	important	unimportant
cover	uncover	kind	unkind
do	undo	lock	unlock
dress	undress	married	unmarried
fortunate	unfortunate	necessary	unnecessary
fortunately	unfortunately	safe	unsafe
happy	unhappy	true	untrue

Circle the letter next to the word that best completes the sentence.

1. The meeting was _____, but we had to go to it.

   a. unkind   c. unhealthy
   b. unimportant   d. untrue

2. The bridge is _____. They have to fix it.

   a. unnecessary   c. unfortunate
   b. unhealthy   d. unsafe

3. Jean was _____ to get the book she wanted.

   a. unable   c. unhappy
   b. unafraid   d. untrue

4. I don't like Amanda. Sometimes she's _____.

   a. unfortunate   c. unkind
   b. unnecessary   d. unsafe

5. Kyle got _____ and went to bed.

    a. unlocked   c. unhappy

    b. undressed   d. unafraid

6. My visit to the doctor was _____. There was nothing wrong with me.

    a. unnecessary   c. unhealthy

    b. unsafe   d. unkind

7. Jeff is 30, rich, and handsome; and he's still _____.

    a. untrue   c. unafraid

    b. unfortunate   d. unmarried

8. I hope you don't believe what Sally said about me. It was _____.

    a. unimportant   c. untrue

    b. unkind   d. unnecessary

USING THE INTERNET TO FIND INFORMATION

1. *Enter the keyword **household poisons** in the search box of any general search engine such as Google or Yahoo. Click on the "search" button or hit "enter" on the keyboard. The search engine will lead you to a list of Web sites.*

   Click on the links to two or three of these Web sites. Look over these sites and choose the one that seems the most interesting and that tells you the most about household poisons. Read a page or two. (Option: write down two or three things you learned about household poisons from this site.)

2. *Enter the keywords **veterinarians, U.S. Department of Labor** in the search box of any general search engine such as Google or Yahoo. Click on the "search" button or hit "enter" on the keyboard. The search engine will lead you to a list of Web sites.*

   Click on the links to two or three of these Web sites. Look over these sites and choose the one that seems the most interesting and that tells you the most about veterinarians. Read a page or two. (Option: write down two or three things you learned about veterinarians from this site.)

CHAPTER 6

Fords, Hondas, and Toyotas

PREVIEW QUESTIONS

Discuss or think about these questions before reading the story.

1. What are the problems with buying a used car? Why do people buy them?

2. About how much does a new family sedan—for example, a Honda Accord, a Toyota Camry, or a Ford Focus—cost?

3. Do all car dealers charge the same price for the same car, or is it possible to get a lower price by shopping around?

Fords, Hondas, and Toyotas

Frank and Sue are going to buy a new car. Their car is 11 years old, and they're having a lot of problems with it; it also needs new tires. **Of course**, they could have it fixed and buy new tires, but that would be **expensive** and a waste of money. They're trying to sell their old car for $300.

They thought about buying a used car to save money, but they decided not to. "If you buy a used car," says Frank, "you're buying another person's problems. We don't want to do that. We want a car that runs well and that we can trust." Naturally a new car will cost a lot, but Frank and Sue are hoping to find one that's not too expensive.

Frank and Sue's **neighbor** Mr. Wallace bought a new Cadillac last month. He's a good friend, and he lets Frank take his car for a ride. It's big and it's beautiful. Mr. Wallace loves it and Frank does, too, but it was very expensive. Mr. Wallace is a lawyer, and he makes a lot of money. He can **afford** a Cadillac, but Frank and Sue can't, so they're looking at Fords, Hondas, and Toyotas.

Every day, Frank and Sue read the car ads in the newspapers. They are also going from dealer to dealer, looking carefully at cars and comparing prices. This takes a lot of time, but they plan to keep their new car for ten years. They know it would be a mistake to **choose** too quickly.

Yesterday they looked at a Honda Accord, and it's **just** what they want. It's not cheap, but it looks nice and has a lot of room and power. People say that it's a great car. Frank and Sue took it for a test drive and they liked it. They plan to buy it.

They're going to the bank today to get a **loan.** It should be easy to get one since they're both working, and they have always paid their bills on time. They have saved some money to buy a car, but they also have to **borrow** $10,000. They're going to pay off the loan in three years.

Answer these questions about the story. *Use your experience and own ideas to answer questions with an asterisk (*). Work in pairs or small groups. The numbers in parentheses tell you which paragraph has the answer.*

1. Why are Frank and Sue buying a new car? (1)

2. Why don't they fix the car they have? (1)

*3. Why do you think it would be a waste of money to fix their car?

4. What does Frank say is the problem with buying a used car? (2)

*5. Do you agree with him? Explain your answer.

6. How do Frank and Mr. Wallace feel about Mr. Wallace's Cadillac? (3)

7. Why can Mr. Wallace afford a Cadillac? (3)

8. Why are Frank and Sue going from dealer to dealer? (4)

9. How long do they plan to keep their new car? (4)

10. Why are they going to buy a Honda Accord? (5)

*11. The Honda Accord is a Japanese car. Do you think that Japanese cars are better than American cars? Explain your answer.

12. Why should it be easy for Frank and Sue to get a car loan? Give two reasons. (6)

GUESSING FROM CONTEXT

Guess the meaning of the key words in these sentences. *Use the context of the story to help you. Circle your answers.*

1. They could have the car fixed and buy new tires, but that would **be expensive.**

   a. be stupid   c. cost a lot
   b. be the best   d. be smart

2. Mr. Wallace is a lawyer and he makes a lot of money. He can **afford** a Cadillac.

   a. rent   c. fix
   b. pay for   d. think about

3. They know it would be a mistake to **choose** too quickly.

   a. go to the bank   c. make a decision
   b. drive   d. ask about the price

WORD ENTRIES

of course / əv kôrs *or* ə-kôrs′ / *idiom:* naturally; certainly; clearly: *Of course I love my children.*

ex·pen·sive / ek-spen′siv / *adjective:* costing a lot: *Hilton hotels are very nice and very **expensive.***

neigh·bor / nā′bər / *noun:* a person who lives near one's house or apartment: *Juanita lives across the street from me. We're **neighbors.***

af·ford / ə-fôrd′ / *verb:* to be able to pay for something (*can* or *can't* usually comes before **afford**): *We're not rich, but we can **afford** a new TV set.*

COMPLETING SENTENCES

Complete the sentences with these words. *Use each word twice. Where a word has different endings, both forms are given.*

neighbor/neighbors	of course	afford	expensive

1. _____ the children want to play.

2. These shoes are _____, but I'm going to buy them.

3. When I was in the hospital, many of my _____ came to see me.

4. It's a beautiful apartment. Do you think we can _____ the rent?

5. This is a gold watch. That's why it's _____.

6. John lives near me, and I know he'll help me. He's a good _____.

7. _____ we're hungry. It's 1:00, and we haven't eaten lunch yet.

8. Dan and Karen want to go to Hawaii, but they can't _____ it.

VOCABULARY FOCUS

choose / chōōz / *verb**: to take one thing or person from two or more; to pick; to select: *The company is going to* **choose** *a new president.*
*The past tense of **choose** is **chose**.

just / just / *adverb*: exactly*: *Kyra looks* **just** *like her mother.*
1: *very recently: We* **just** *got home.* **2**: only: *I was* **just** *trying to help you.*
*The adverb **just** has other meanings.

loan / lōn / *noun*: money or anything that a person is given and must pay or give back: *Stacy went to the bank to ask for a* **loan**. *She needs $3,000.* —*verb*: to give money that must be paid back; to give anything that must be returned: *I'll* **loan** *the book to you. But don't forget to return it.*

bor·row / bor′ō or bôr′ō / *verb*: to receive money that must be paid back; to receive or take anything that must be returned*: *May I* **borrow** *$30 from you? I'll pay it back tomorrow.*
*To *loan* is to give; to *borrow* is to take.

COMPLETING SENTENCES

Complete the sentences with these words. *Use each word twice. Where a word has different endings, both forms are given.*

borrow/borrowed	just	loan/loaned	choose/chose

1. The money I got from Bill wasn't a gift. It was a _____.

2. Steve _____ his cousin's car to drive to the airport.

3. Erica likes the college she _____, and she's doing very well.

4. I asked Charley to write a report, and he did it _____ the way I wanted.

5. It's important to _____ friends carefully.

6. I _____ my bike to Jim this morning; I hope he takes good care of it.

7. Your son and mine are _____ about the same age.

8. May I _____ your pen for a minute?

Discuss or think about these questions before completing the story that follows.

1. About how much do you think it costs to go to a public college for a year?

2. About how much do you think it costs to go to a private college for a year?

3. If your family doesn't have much money, how can you get money to pay for college?

Complete the story with these words

of course	afford	loan	neighbors
borrow	just	choose	expensive

Paying for College

Marissa and Carmen live on the same block. They're _____ and best friends. "We do so much together; we're _____ like sisters," they say.

Marissa and Carmen are seniors at George Washington High School, and they want to go to college next year. _____ it is _____ to go to college. And their families don't have much money. They can't _____ to pay for their daughters' college education.

Marissa and Carmen are going to _____ a state college because it costs less. They'll also have to _____ money to pay for college. Next week they're going to apply for a _____ from a bank.

Discuss these questions and topics in pairs or small groups.

1. Complete the following sentence. **Of course** I like to _____ _____.

2. Name a store where you can buy clothing that's not **expensive**. Where can you eat out that's not expensive?

3. Are most of your **neighbors** friendly? How well do you know your neighbors?

4. Imagine that someone gave you a million dollars. What would you buy that you can't **afford** now?

5. If you had to **choose** between being very rich or very smart, what **choice** would you make? Explain your answer.

6. Look at your watch or a clock and complete the following sentence. It's **just** _____.

7. Did you ever **loan** money to a friend or relative? Did you get it back?

8. Did you ever **borrow** money from a bank or from a friend? Why did you borrow it?

WORD FAMILIES

Complete the sentences with these words. *If necessary, add an ending to the word so it forms a correct sentence.* (adj. = adjective and adv. = adverb)

1. **expensive** (adj.)   **expense** (noun)

   A. Food is a big _____ for all families.

   B. I love to travel, but it's _____.

2. **neighbor** (noun)   **neighborhood** (noun)

   A. It's a pretty _____ with tall trees and nice homes.

   B. Mrs. Johnson sold her house. We'll be getting new _____.

3. **to afford** (verb)   **affordable** (adj.)

   A. We want to buy a house, but it's hard to find one that's _____.

   B. That coat is beautiful, but I can't _____ it.

4. **to choose** (verb)   **choice** (noun)

   A. I like the red sweater and the blue one. I don't know which one to _____.

   B. We have to pay taxes. We have no _____.

BUILDING ADJECTIVES WITH –*ABLE*

The suffix -***able*** is added to some verbs and nouns to form an adjective. -***Able*** usually means *able to be* or *likely to.* For example, *wash + able = washable,* which means *able to be washed; change + able = changeable,* which means *likely to change.*

-***Able*** can also mean *having* or *giving,* for example, *value + able = valuable,* which means *having value; comfort + able = comfortable,* which means *giving comfort.*

Verb or Noun	Adjective	Verb or Noun	Adjective
accept	acceptable	pay	payable
afford	affordable	return	returnable
change	changeable	understand	understandable
comfort	comfortable	use	usable
control	controllable	value	valuable
enjoy	enjoyable	wash	washable
like	likable	work	workable
move	movable		

Circle the letter next to the word that best completes the sentence.

1. Kelly is very _____. You never know what's she going to do next.

   a. valuable
   b. changeable
   c. comfortable
   d. likable

2. Everyone liked the show. It was _____.

   a. controllable
   b. usable
   c. acceptable
   d. enjoyable

3. The empty soda bottles are _____. We can bring them to the store and get money for them.

   a. washable
   b. affordable
   c. returnable
   d. likable

4. The teachers thought they had a good plan, but the principal said it wasn't _____.

   a. acceptable
   b. enjoyable
   c. changeable
   d. comfortable

5. The desk is big and heavy, but it's _____.

   a. washable
   b. likable
   c. controllable
   d. movable

6. The jacket is _____, but use warm water, not hot.

   a. acceptable
   b. washable
   c. affordable
   d. returnable

7. There was a fire in our apartment building. Fortunately, it was
   _____, and the firefighters put it out.

    a. controllable   c. workable

    b. movable   d. changeable

8. Jay's pay is low and he works long hours. His desire for a better job
   is _____.

    a. acceptable   c. understandable

    b. usable   d. acceptable

READING CAR ADS

When Frank and Sue decided to buy a new car, they started to read the car ads in the newspaper. But that wasn't easy. The biggest problem was the large number of abbreviations in the ads. Here are some abbreviations they saw.

Abbreviation	Meaning
1. dr.	door
2. cyl. or V	cylinder
3. auto or auto trans.	automatic transmission
4. man. or man. trans.	manual transmission
5. cruise	cruise control—it enables a car to maintain the same speed automatically
6. air or a/c or air cond.	air-conditioning
7. AM/FM st., AM/FM st. cass.	AM/FM stereo; AM/FM stereo cassette
8. CD	CD player
9. P/S, P/B; or p/s/b; or psb	power steering and power brakes
10. P/W, P/L, P/M; or P/winds/lks/mirrs	power windows, locks, and mirrors
11. ABS or ABS brks	antilock braking system
12. VIN	vehicle identification number—This number is used to identify the car on all paperwork.
13. MSPR	manufacturer's suggested retail price—The price the manufacturer *suggests* to the dealer. By law the MSRP is placed on the window of all new cars.
14. in stk.	in stock

Now read two of the ads Frank and Sue saw. Then answer the questions about them.

A.
> **New Honda Accord EX**
> 4 Dr., 4 Cyl., Auto, A/C
> PS, PB, ABS, PW, PL, PM
> Cruise, AM/FM st./CD
> Vin# 4A30660
> MSPR $23,990

1. Does this car have air-conditioning?
2. What type of transmission does it have?
3. How many doors?
4. Does it have cruise control?
5. How many cylinders does it have?
6. What kind of radio does it have? Does it have a CD player?
7. What does the ad tell you about its steering and brakes?
8. What does it tell you about its windows and locks?
9. What's the car's vehicle identification number?
10. What's the price suggested by Honda?

B.
> **Used Car**
> '03 Ford Taurus $8,995
> V6, Auto Trans., AC
> P/S, P/B, ABS, P/W, P/L
> AM/FM/CD 31,305 miles
> VIN# 3G245707

1. Does this Taurus have air-conditioning?
2. How many miles has it gone?
3. Does it have power steering and brakes?
4. Does it have power windows and locks?
5. Does it have an antilock braking system?
6. How many cylinders does it have?

7. Is the transmission manual or automatic?

8. Does it have a CD player?

9. What is its vehicle identification number?

10. Why doesn't the ad give an MSRP?

ACTIVITY

Look at the car ads in a newspaper. *Bring two of the ads to class. Copy one of them on the board, and ask another student in the class to read it.*

USING THE INTERNET TO FIND INFORMATION

1. *Enter* the keyword **Honda Accord** *in the search box of any general search engine such as Google or Yahoo. Click on the "search" button or hit "enter" on the keyboard. The search engine will lead you to a list of Web sites.*

   Click on the links to two or three of these Web sites. Look over these sites and choose the one that seems the most interesting and that tells you the most about a Honda Accord. Read a page or two. (Option: Write down two or three things you learned about a Honda Accord from this site.)

2. *Enter* the keyword **Toyota Camry** *in the search box of any general search engine such as Google or Yahoo. Click on the "search" button or hit "enter" on the keyboard. The search engine will lead you to a list of Web sites.*

   Click on the links to two or three of these Web sites. Look over these sites and choose the one that seems the most interesting and that tells you the most about a Toyota Camry. Read a page or two. (Option: write down two or three things you learned about a Toyota Camry from this site.)

SYNONYMS

Next to each sentence, write the word that has the same meaning or almost the same meaning as the part of the sentence in bold print.

bit	fortunate	exploring	hates
just	burning	improving	both

1. _____ My job pays well and I was **lucky** to get it.

2. _____ My dog **doesn't like** baths.

3. _____ Julio's car is **on fire.**

4. _____ Cristina put a **small amount** of milk and sugar in her tea.

5. _____ Doug is a good tennis player, and he's **getting better.**

6. _____ It's **exactly** five o'clock. Time to go home.

7. _____ Marina and her sister are happy it's snowing. **The two** of them like to ski.

8. _____ The company is **looking carefully at** ways to cut expenses.

SENTENCE COMPLETION

Complete the sentences with these words.

choose	neighbors	swallow	share
rushing	proud	wipe	poisonous

1. Brad is late. He's _____ to get to class before the bell rings.

2. My bike got wet in the rain. I have to _____ it off.

3. This menu is so large I don't know what to _____.

4. Kate is _____ of her beautiful garden.

5. Married couples _____ their lives.

6. Tiffany lives around the corner from us. We're _____.

7. Some cleaning fluids and powders are _____.

8. The soup is too hot to _____.

Complete the story with these words.

borrow	fun	afford	still
mistake	expensive	loan	of course

A Boat

Carl and Michelle are married and live in Dallas, Texas. In the summer they rent a home on a large lake because they like to get away from the heat of the city and go swimming. Now Carl wants to buy a boat, but Michelle says that boats are too _____ and they can't _____ one.

Carl wants to _____ the money for the boat. Michelle knows they can get a _____ from the bank, but she _____ doesn't like the idea. She thinks it would be a _____ to pay so much for something they don't need.

Carl says, "_____ we don't need a boat, but my business is doing well, and it would be a lot of _____ to have one."

Two Young Men

CHAPTER 7

Working and Swimming

PREVIEW QUESTIONS

Discuss or think about these questions before reading the story.

1. Do you like to read? What do you like to read? Do you like to study? Do you like school? Explain your answer.

2. How interested are you in sports? What's your favorite sport?

3. Do you think high-school students should work in the summer? Explain your answer. What kinds of jobs can they get?

Working and Swimming

Pete and Tom are brothers. Pete's 18 and he'll graduate from high school in June. He's a good student and **spends** a lot of time reading and studying. Last year he had a B **average,** and this year he's getting all As. Math is his favorite subject, but he also likes English and history. He plans to go to college in September and will have no trouble getting into a good college. Pete's shy and quiet.

Tom's 16 and he hates school. He has only a C average, and he doesn't like to study or read. He **prefers** to play basketball or watch TV. He's good at all sports, especially basketball. Tom likes to talk and has a lot of friends. He's also handsome, dresses well, and is a good dancer. He's very popular with the girls.

In the summer, Pete works at a gas station. He likes the work, especially when he gets the chance to fix cars. He loves cars and is learning a lot from the owner of the gas station, who's an excellent mechanic. Pete saves the money he makes to help pay for his college education. His parents don't have a lot of money, and going to college is expensive.

Tom works at Burger King during the summer. "It's not great work," he says, "and I don't get paid much. But I'm happy to be working and making some money. It's not easy for a high-school student to get a summer job." Some of Tom's friends don't work in the summer and don't want to. But he likes to work and he likes the money.

In the evening, Tom plays basketball in the park with his friends. Pete usually stays home and reads or watches TV, but sometimes he goes out with his friends. On Saturday and Sunday afternoon, Pete and Tom go swimming in a **pool** near their home. Pete's only an average swimmer, but Tom's very good.

Pete and Tom have to pay to get into the pool, but it's big and they have a lot of fun with their friends. Tom likes to **dive** and swim in the **deep** end of the pool. Pete prefers to go into the **shallow** end. He can't dive well. Pete and Tom swim or sit on the **edge** of the pool until they get tired, and then they walk home. It's a nice way to spend a summer afternoon.

Answer these questions about the story. *Use your experience and own ideas to answer questions with an asterisk (*). Work in pairs or small groups. The numbers in parentheses tell you which paragraph in the story has the answer.*

1. How does Pete spend much of his time? (1)

2. What does he plan to do in September? (1)

3. Name three things Tom likes to do. (2)

4. How are Pete and Tom different? (1,2)

*5. Are boys who are good at sports usually popular with girls? If so, why?

6. What does Pete like to do at the gas station? (3)

7. Why is he learning a lot from the owner of the gas station? (3)

*8. Do you think Pete can get financial aid to go to college? If so, why?

9. Why is Tom happy to be working? Give two reasons. (4)

10. What do Pete and Tom do on Saturday and Sunday? (5)

11. What end of the pool does Tom like to go into? And Pete? Why does Pete go into that end of the pool? (6)

*12. Who do you think has more fun at the pool—Tom or Pete? Explain your answer.

Guess the meaning of the key words in these sentences. *Use the context of the story to help you. Circle your answers.*

1. Pete is a good student and **spends a lot of time** reading and studying.

   a. wastes a lot of time   c. doesn't like

   b. enjoys   d. uses a lot of time

2. Tom **prefers to** play basketball or watch TV.

   a. has to   c. tries to

   b. likes to . . . better   d. is afraid to

3. Tom likes to **dive** and swim in the deep end of the pool.

   a. jump head first into the water   c. run into the water

   b. walk quickly into the water   d. walk slowly into the water

WORD ENTRIES

> **spend** / spend / *verb** **1**: to use money to buy something: *Clara **spends** a lot of money on clothes.* **2**: *to use time: Frank **spent** 40 minutes washing his car.*
> *The past tense of **spend** is **spent**.
>
> **av·er·age** / av'rij / *noun*: the result of adding several numbers, for example, test scores, and then dividing the sum by how many numbers were added: *I got 65, 85, and 90 on my tests this marking period. My **average** is 80.*
> —*adjective*: ordinary: *Megan is an **average** cook. She's not great and she's not bad.*
> —*verb*: to do or have an average: *We **averaged** 55 miles per hour on our trip to Virginia.*
>
> **pre·fer** / pri-fûr' / *verb*: to like better: *Sometimes I drink tea, but I **prefer** coffee.*
>
> **pool**/ pōol / *noun* **1**: a small area of still water: *The rain was heavy, and now there are **pools** of water on the field.* **2**: a small area of water for swimming: *I want to stay at a hotel that has a **pool**.*

COMPLETING SENTENCES

Complete the sentences with these words. *Use each word twice. Where a word has different endings, both forms are given.*

average/averaging	spending/spent	pool	prefer/prefers

1. Chelsea _____ $60 at the supermarket.

2. I like to go to the movies, but my wife _____ to stay home and watch TV.

3. Andrea isn't your _____ lawyer. She's one of the best.

4. There's a _____ of water on the bathroom floor.

5. We can fly to Chicago or go by train. Which do you _____?

6. I hear our new high school is going to have a _____. That's great!

7. Eric is _____ the evening at his friend's house.

8. Mark is the best basketball player on his team. He's _____ 20 points a game.

WORD ENTRIES

> **dive** / dīv / *verb*:* to jump head first into water: *Keith is **diving** into the lake.*
> —*noun:* a head-first jump into water: *Pam made a beautiful **dive** into the pool.*
> *The past tense of **dive** is **dived** or **dove**.
>
> **deep** / dēp / *adjective:* going far down or into: *The middle of the lake is very **deep**.*
> —*adverb:* far down or into: *The U.S. army moved **deep** into Iraq.*
>
> **shal·low** / shal'ō / *adjective:* not far from top to bottom; not deep: *It's all right for Bobby to go into the pool. It's **shallow**.*
>
> **edge** / ej / *noun:* the area where an object ends: *Oscar is sitting on the **edge** of the bed, putting on his shoes.*

COMPLETING SENTENCES

Complete the sentences with these words. *Use each word twice. Where a word has different endings, both forms are given.*

shallow	dive/diving	edge	deep

1. Alex is afraid to _____ into the water. He can't swim well.

2. That's a very _____ cut. I'm taking you to the hospital.

3. The books fell off the _____ of the desk.

4. The road is covered with water, but it's _____. We can drive through it.

5. It's been snowing hard for 24 hours. The snow is _____.

6. You're driving too close to the _____ of the road.

7. Jamal is _____ into the river.

8. The lake is small, and it's too _____ to swim in.

Discuss or think about these questions before completing the story that follows.

1. Can you swim? Are you a good swimmer?
2. Do you swim much? Where do you swim?
3. Why is it good to know how to swim?

Complete the story with these words.

edge	shallow	spend	dive
deep	prefer	average	pool

Swimming in the River

Diana and her brother, Todd, like to swim. Sometimes they go to a state park where there is a _____, but they have to drive ten miles to get there. They _____ to swim in a river near their house. They can walk there in five minutes.

They like to _____ into the water from the _____ of the river and swim until it's time to go home. In July and August, when the weather is hot and the days are long, they _____ hours swimming in the cool water.

Although the river is _____ where they go swimming, they aren't afraid. Diana is an excellent swimmer, and Todd is above _____. Parts of the river are _____ and very safe, but they don't like to swim there. It's not as much fun.

Discuss these questions and topics in pairs or small groups.

1. Do you **spend** a lot of time watching TV? Talking on the phone? Listening to music?

2. Carlos got 90, 70, 55, and 85 on his math tests. What is his **average** on those tests?

3. Complete this sentence. I like _____, but I **prefer** _____.

4. Do you think it's more fun to swim in the ocean or in a **pool**? Why? Which is safer?

5. **Divers** explore the ocean. Some divers look for ships that are at the bottom of the sea. What famous ship did divers find in the Atlantic Ocean in 1989? The name of the ship begins with a *T*.

6. Most people have a **deep** interest in something, such as politics, movies, clothes, sports, or history. Name something you're **deeply** interested in.

7. Abraham Lincoln was a deep thinker. He was able to understand difficult ideas. What do we mean when we say that a person is a **shallow** thinker?

8. Many people are afraid to stand near the **edge** of a high roof or bridge. They're afraid of heights. Are you?

Complete the sentences with these words. *If necessary, add an ending to the word so it forms a correct sentence.* (adj. = adjective and adv. = adverb)

1. **to prefer** (verb)　　　　**preference** (noun)　　　　**preferable** (adj.)

   A. If you have the money, buying a house is _____ to renting.

   B. I like country music, but my son _____ rock.

   C. We have vanilla, chocolate, and strawberry ice cream. What's your _____?

2. **to dive** (verb) **diver** (noun)

   A. I love to watch the _____ in the Olympic Games.

   B. It's not safe to _____ into this pool. It's too shallow.

3. **deep** (adj.) **deeply** (adv.) **to deepen** (verb)

   A. Pedro and Vanessa are _____ in love.

   B. They're going to _____ the lake so people can swim in it.

   C. The trunk of the car is _____. We can get a lot in it.

BUILDING ADJECTIVES AND NOUNS WITH -*FUL*

The suffix -***ful*** is added to nouns to form an adjective. For example, *power + ful = powerful; beauty + ful = beautiful; help + ful = helpful.*

-***Ful*** usually means *full of* or *having a lot of,* or *giving. Powerful* means *full of power; beautiful* means *having a lot of beauty; helpful* means *giving help.*

Noun	Adjective	Noun	Adjective
beauty	beautiful	peace	peaceful
care	careful	power	powerful
color	colorful	rest	restful
fear	fearful	thought	thoughtful
help	helpful	use	useful
hope	hopeful	waste	wasteful
joy	joyful	youth	youthful

Circle the letter next to the word that best completes the sentence.

1. The book was very _____. It helped me a lot.

   a. fearful   c. colorful

   b. useful   d. youthful

2. Lillian never drives fast. She's a _____ driver.

   a. joyful   c. peaceful

   b. powerful   d. careful

3. Thinking about war and nuclear bombs makes us _____.

    a. fearful   c. powerful

    b. useful   d. restful

4. It's _____ to cook more than your family will eat.

    a. thoughtful   c. wasteful

    b. helpful   d. colorful

5. Life in the country is more _____ than life in the city.

    a. useful   c. powerful

    b. careful   d. peaceful

6. I'm not sure I'll get the job, but I'm _____.

    a. hopeful   c. thoughtful

    b. colorful   d. helpful

7. Greg is 40, but he's still _____.

    a. careful   c. youthful

    b. fearful   d. wasteful

8. It's fall and the leaves on the trees are _____.

    a. powerful   c. helpful

    b. colorful   d. useful

1. *Enter the keywords **auto mechanics, U.S. Department of Labor** in the search box of any general search engine such as Google or Yahoo. Click on the "search" button or hit "enter" on the keyboard. The search engine will lead you to a list of Web sites.*

   Click on the links to two or three of these Web sites. Look over these sites and choose the one that seems the most interesting and that tells you the most about auto mechanics. Read a page or two. (Option: write down two or three things you learned about auto mechanics from this site.)

2. *Enter the keywords **service station attendants** in the search box of any general search engine such as Google or Yahoo. Click on the "search" button or hit "enter" on the keyboard. The search engine will lead you to a list of Web sites.*

   Click on the links to two or three of these Web sites. Look over these sites and choose the one that seems the most interesting and that tells you the most about service station attendants. Read a page or two. (Option: write down two or three things you learned about service station attendants from this site.)

CHAPTER 8

Hunting

Discuss or think about these questions before reading the story.

1. Some people think it's OK to hunt. Others say it's wrong to kill animals for sport. What do you think? Explain your answer.

2. Have you ever gone hunting? Do you know anyone who likes to hunt?

3. Why do people like to hunt?

Hunting

Pete and Tom hate to see the summer end. The day after Labor Day, the pool closes and they have to go back to school. That's no fun. It's especially hard on Tom, but Pete also misses the pool and his work at the gas station.

There's one thing that Pete and Tom like about the fall. They love to **hunt.** When Tom was in the eighth grade and Pete was in high school, their father taught them how to hunt. But their mother didn't like the idea one bit. "I don't think anyone should **shoot** animals," she said. "Killing is never right." And of course she was also afraid that her sons might get hurt. She still tells them to be careful when they go hunting.

On Saturdays in the fall, Pete and Tom get up at 6:00 and spend the day hunting. Their father owns a small Ford truck, and he lets them borrow it to drive to the woods that are about 20 miles from their house. The woods are a great place to hunt, and they're also very beautiful when the leaves change colors in the fall.

Last Saturday Pete and Tom were walking in the woods with their rifles when they saw a deer drinking from a **stream.** They were hunting for rabbits and were surprised and happy to see the deer. It was almost too beautiful to shoot. They moved closer. They **hesitated** for a minute. Should they shoot the deer or let it go? Then Tom **aimed** his rifle at the deer and shot. Tom's aim is very good; he didn't miss.

This was the first time they ever shot a deer. They were happy and sad at the same time. They remembered their mother's words about killing. They went over to the deer. It was a **huge** animal. They tried to **lift** it, but it was too heavy. They had to **drag** it on the ground to their truck; it wasn't far.

Some **hunters** congratulated them and helped them lift the deer into the truck. Then Tom and Pete put their rifles next to the deer and started home. "I can't wait to show the deer to Dad," Tom said. "He'll be proud of us."

TRUE OR FALSE

If the sentence is true, write *T*. If it's false, write *F*.

_____ 1. Tom and Pete go back to school on Labor Day.

_____ 2. It's especially hard for Tom to return to school.

_____ 3. Pete and Tom's mother was happy that they learned to hunt.

_____ 4. On Saturdays in the fall, Pete and Tom get up early to go hunting.

_____ 5. Their father drives them to the woods.

_____ 6. Pete and Tom were surprised and happy to see the deer.

_____ 7. Tom shot the deer immediately.

_____ 8. Some hunters helped lift the deer into the truck.

WHAT DO YOU THINK?

Use your experience, judgment, and the story to answer these questions.

1. Why was going back to school especially hard for Tom?

2. Sometimes hunters accidentally shoot other hunters. What can hunters do to protect themselves?

3. Why were Pete and Tom happy that they shot the deer? Why do you think they were also sad?

4. What do you think their father said when he saw the deer? And their mother?

GUESSING FROM CONTEXT

Guess the meaning of the key words in these sentences. *Use the context of the story to help you. Circle your answers.*

1. Pete and Tom love to **hunt.**

   a. feed animals

   b. take pictures of animals

   c. look for animals to kill or capture

   d. watch animals

2. Pete and Tom moved closer to the deer. They **hesitated** for a minute.

    a. talked   c. were quiet

    b. were happy   d. stopped

3. Pete and Tom went over to the deer. It was a **huge** animal.

    a. very beautiful   c. very nice

    b. very large   d. very small

MINI-DICTIONARY—PART ONE

WORD ENTRIES

hunt / hunt / *verb* **1**: to look for animals to kill or capture: *Victor and his cousin John like to* **hunt** *ducks.* **2**: to look carefully for something: *Peggy is* **hunting** *for a job.* —*noun*: the act of hunting: *Ryan is going to a* **hunt**. *That's why he has a rifle in the trunk of his car.*

hun·ter / hun'tər / *noun*: a person who hunts: *The fox is running away from the* **hunters** *and the dogs.*

shoot / sho͞ot / *verb*:* to hit, or try to hit, someone or something, with a bullet from a gun: *The man who robbed the bank had a gun in his hand, but he didn't* **shoot** *anyone.*
*The past tense of **shoot** is **shot**.

stream / strēm / *noun* **1**: a body of water that flows, especially a small one: *We sat on the side of the* **stream** *and put our feet into the water.* **2**: anything that flows continuously: *It was 5:00 P.M., and a* **stream** *of people was coming out of the train station.* —*verb*: to flow continuously: *Water was* **streaming** *from the broken pipe.*

hes·i·tate / hez'ə-tāt / *verb* **1**: to stop briefly before or during an action: *Nick* **hesitated** *before he answered my question.* **2**: to be slow or unwilling to act or decide: *I* **hesitated** *to phone my friend. It was very late.*

COMPLETING SENTENCES

Complete the sentences with these words. *Use each word twice. Where a word has different endings, both forms are given.*

stream	hesitates/hesitated	hunt/hunting	shoot/shot

1. I _____ to ask my sister for a loan, but I needed the money.

2. Lee Harvey Oswald _____ President John Kennedy in Dallas, Texas, on November 22, 1963.

3. There are no fish in the _____. It's too shallow.

4. You need a license to _____.

5. The police officer told the man to stop, or he would _____.

6. Melissa thinks her salary is too low, but she _____ to quit her job.

7. Kevin and Patricia are _____ for an apartment. They want to move.

8. It's three o'clock, and a _____ of students is coming out of school.

MINI-DICTIONARY—PART TWO

WORD ENTRIES

aim / ām / *verb* **1:** to point a gun or other thing at a person or object: *The soldier* **aimed** *his rifle at the enemy.* **2:** to plan to do something: *Our company* **aims** *to make more money next year.* —*noun:* **1:** the act of aiming: *Police officers practice shooting to improve their* **aim**. **2:** what one wishes to do; a plan: *What are the* **aims** *of the president's trip to Europe?*

huge / hyōōj *or* yōōj / *adjective:* very large: *Lake Champlain is 121 miles long. It's* **huge**.

lift / lift / *verb:* to raise something to a higher level: *I want to move this desk. Can you help me* **lift** *it?*

drag / drag / *verb:* to pull along on a surface: *Brittany is* **dragging** *a big box out of the closet.*

COMPLETING SENTENCES

Complete the sentences with these words. *Use each word twice. Where a word has different endings, both forms are given.*

lift/lifts	drag/dragging	huge	aim/aims

1. One of the _____ of the space program was to land an astronaut on the moon.
2. The baby is _____ her doll behind her.
3. There are many _____ buildings in Chicago.
4. The suitcases are light. They'll be easy to _____.
5. Canada is larger than the United States. It's a _____ country.
6. I told my son I would _____ him out of bed if he didn't get up soon.
7. Kareem is strong. He _____ weights every day.
8. My brother and I own a clothing store, and we _____ to please our customers.

STORY COMPLETION

Discuss or think about these questions before completing the story that follows.

1. Have you ever gone camping? Would you like to?
2. Have you ever seen a bear other than in a zoo or circus? If so, where?
3. Many bears look friendly. Is it safe to feed or go near them? Explain your answer.

Complete the story with these words.

huge	dragged	hunt	aim
shoot	hesitate	lift	stream

A Hungry Bear

Scott, Lisa, and their two children love the outdoors. One summer they were camping near a _____ in Acadia National Park in Maine. No one is allowed to _____ in the park, but Scott had his rifle with him. He never thought he would have to use it, but he felt safer with it.

81

Their youngest child, Jessica, was playing outside their tent when a _____ bear came looking for food. Scott got his rifle, and when he saw that the bear was getting close to Jessica, he didn't _____ to _____ and kill the bear. Scott's _____ is very good.

Jessica ran into the tent crying. Her mother hugged her and told her everything was OK. Scott went over to the bear. It was too heavy to _____, so they _____ it away from the tent and left it under a tree.

SHARING INFORMATION

Discuss these questions and topics in pairs or small groups.

1. We have laws that limit when people can **hunt** and the number of animals a **hunter** can kill. Why are these laws necessary?

2. Thousands of people are **shot** and killed in the United States every year. Do you think we need stricter laws to control guns? Explain your answer.

3. The word **stream** usually refers to water, but it can also refer to other things, for example, a stream of people or a stream of questions. What do we mean by a stream of people? A stream of questions?

4. Complete sentence A or B. A. I **hesitated** to _____.
   B. I **hesitated** before _____.

5. Everyone needs to have **aims**—things they plan or are trying to do. Name one of your aims. Why are aims important in life?

6. There are many problems in the world. Some are small; others are **huge**. Name one of the huge ones.

7. Name some things that are heavy and difficult to **lift**. Name some that are light and easy to lift.

8. When time seems to move slowly, we say it **drags**. Does time ever drag for you? If so, when?

WORD FAMILIES

Complete the sentences with these words. *If necessary, add an ending to the word so it forms a correct sentence.* (adj. = adjective and adv. = adverb)

1. **to hunt** (verb) **hunter** (noun) **hunting** (noun)

   A. _____ get a lot of fresh air and exercise.

   B. _____ and fishing are popular sports.

   C. Most African countries don't allow anyone to _____ elephants.

2. **to shoot** (verb) **shot** (noun)

   A. When I saw that the man had a gun, I said, "Take my watch and wallet, but don't _____."

   B. Someone tried to kill Henry, but the _____ missed.

3. **to hesitate** (verb) **hesitant** (adj.)

   hesitantly (adv.) **hesitation** (noun)

   A. Ashley _____ told her father about her accident.

   B. We _____ to go swimming; the water was cold.

   C. I had no _____ asking my friend for a dollar.

   D. We knew Allison's son was taking drugs, but we were _____ to tell her.

BUILDING ADJECTIVES WITH -*LESS*

The suffix *-less* is added to nouns to form an adjective. For example, *power + less = powerless; fear + less = fearless.*

The suffix *-less* means *having no* or *without*. *Powerless* means *having no power* or *without power; fearless* means *having no fear* or *without fear.*

Noun	Adjective	Noun	Adjective
aim	aimless	need	needless
care	careless	power	powerless
end	endless	sleep	sleepless
fear	fearless	speech	speechless
help	helpless	sugar	sugarless
home	homeless	use	useless
hope	hopeless	weight	weightless

Circle the letter next to the word that best completes the sentence.

1. I buy _____ gum. It's better for my teeth.

   a. weightless   c. useless

   b. sugarless   d. powerless

2. Fred made some _____ mistakes on his math exam.

   a. hopeless   c. fearless

   b. aimless   d. careless

3. Denise is very tired. She had a (an) _____ night.

   a. endless   c. sleepless

   b. useless   d. speechless

4. Does the city have a place where _____ people can stay?

   a. homeless   c. powerless

   b. careless   d. aimless

5. The movie was too long. It seemed _____.

   a. hopeless   c. endless

   b. useless   d. helpless

6. Victoria will make a good soldier. She's _____.

   a. careless   c. weightless

   b. fearless   d. aimless

7. This clock is _____. It won't run.

   a. needless   c. endless

   b. helpless   d. useless

8. Everything in outerspace is _____.

   a. weightless   c. powerless

   b. aimless   d. speechless

1. *Enter* the keyword **against hunting** *in the search box of any general search engine such as Google or Yahoo. Click on the "search" button or hit "enter" on the keyboard. The search engine will lead you to a list of Web sites.*

   Click on the links to two or three of these Web sites. Look over these sites and choose the one that seems the most interesting and that tells you the most about why we should not hunt. Read a page or two. (Option: write down two or three reasons against hunting that you learned from this site.)

2. *Enter* the keyword **Labor Day** *in the search box of any general search engine such as Google or Yahoo. Click on the "search" button or hit "enter" on the keyboard. The search engine will lead you to a list of Web sites.*

   Click on the links to two or three of these Web sites. Look over these sites and choose the one that seems the most interesting and that tells you the most about Labor Day. Read a page or two. (Option: write down two or three things you learned about Labor Day from this site.)

CHAPTER 9

A Bitter Argument

PREVIEW QUESTIONS

Discuss or think about these questions before reading the story.

1. Many students leave high school before they graduate. We say they drop out of school. Is it easy or difficult for these students to get good jobs? Explain your answer.

2. Why do students drop out of school?

3. What can high schools do to help students stay in school and graduate? What can parents do?

A Bitter Argument

Tom and Pete live in New York State, where you have to go to school until you're 16. Then you're free to **quit.** Tom's just 16 and he wants to quit school and go to work. However, his teachers and counselor know that to get a good job, he will need **at least** a high-school education. They want him to stay in school and to graduate.

Tom likes his science class, but he thinks that all of his other classes are a waste of time. He says they're **dull** and that he's not learning anything in them. His teachers say that he's a nice person, but that he's lazy and doesn't study. He says he doesn't want to study. He wants to get a full-time job and **earn** some money. "Why does everyone have to go to school and study?" he asks. "Thomas Edison never finished the first grade, and he did all right for himself."

Tom's parents also want him to stay in school. They think it would be **foolish** for him to quit. "All of the other boys and girls in the neighborhood plan to finish high school," his mother said to him. "And no one is going to give you a good job if you don't have a high-school diploma. You're no Tom Edison. Why don't you finish high school and then look for a job?"

Tom doesn't care what the other kids are doing. "I want to be myself, and I want to go to work now," he said to his mother. "Look, I'm 16 and I'm not a baby anymore. You have to let me grow up. You know I hate school."

"I know," she replied, "that there are a lot of things in life that we hate and that we have to do. If you quit school now, you're running away from your problems, and that's no way to grow up."

Last night, Tom and his mother had another **argument** about his plan to quit school. She **shouted** at him and he shouted back at her. They **argued** for almost an hour. She said he would be a **fool** to quit school. He said he didn't want to hear any more about school and what his friends were doing. It was a **bitter** argument. Will Tom listen to his mother, or will he quit school?

Answer these questions about the story. *Use your experience and own ideas to answer questions with an asterisk (*). Work in pairs or small groups. The numbers in parentheses show which paragraph in the story has the answer.*

1. At what age can you quit school in New York? (1)

2. Why do Tom's teachers and counselor want him to stay in school? (1)

*3. Why do you think Tom likes his science class?

4. Why does he think that most of his classes are a waste of time? (2)

*5. What do you think makes a class dull? What makes a class interesting?

6. What do Tom's teachers say about him? (2)

7. What do his parents think of his quitting school? (3)

8. What does his mother say about the other boys and girls in the neighborhood? (3)

9. What does Tom say he wants? (4)

10. How does his mother reply? (5)

11. What did Tom and his mother argue about last night? (6)

*12. Do you think he'll listen to his mother, or will he quit school? Explain your answer.

WORD GUESSING

Guess the meaning of the key words in these sentences. *Use the context of the story to help you. Circle your answers.*

1. Tom's parents think it would be **foolish** for him to quit.

   a. a good idea   c. necessary
   b. stupid   d. preferable

2. Tom's mother **shouted at him** and he shouted back at her.

   a. spoke to him in a loud voice   c. spoke to him in a quiet voice
   b. corrected him   d. laughed at him

3. It was a **bitter** argument.

   a. long   c. friendly
   b. very interesting   d. very unpleasant

WORD ENTRIES

> **quit** / kwit / *verb*:* to stop doing something; to leave a job or school: *I know smoking is a bad habit, but it's difficult to* **quit**.
> *The past tense of **quit** is **quit**.
>
> **at least** / at lēst / *idiom* **1:** a minimum of; maybe more, but not less: *A new refrigerator will cost* **at least** *$300.* **2:** "but the good thing is": *Our new boss is strict, but* **at least** *she listens.*
>
> **dull** / dul / *adjective* **1:** not interesting: *I didn't finish the book. It was* **dull**. **2:** not sharp: *These knives are* **dull**. *They won't cut the steak.*
>
> **earn** / ûrn / *verb* **1:** to receive money for doing work: *Luz has a good job. She* **earns** *$65,000 a year.* **2:** to receive something you deserve because of what you did: *Our history teacher gives good marks only to those who* **earn** *them.*

COMPLETING SENTENCES

Complete the sentences with these words. *Use each word twice. Where a word has different endings, both forms are given.*

dull	at least	earn/earned	quit/quits

1. I was going _____ 70 miles an hour when the police officer stopped me.

2. Audrey never _____ trying. She'll do well in life.

3. We left before the end of the game. It was _____.

4. Most doctors _____ a lot of money.

5. Jeff _____ the baseball team because he wasn't playing much.

6. These scissors are _____. I'm going to buy a better pair.

7. It was cloudy the day we had our picnic, but _____ it didn't rain.

8. The soldiers fought bravely. They _____ their medals.

WORD ENTRIES

> **fool** / fōōl / *noun:* a stupid person: *Donna was a **fool** to marry Lee. He's lazy and he drinks too much.* —*verb* **1:** to make a person think something is true when it isn't: *We thought Mickey was telling the truth, but he wasn't. He **fooled** us.* **2:** to joke; to kid: *Valerie was **fooling**; she wasn't serious.*
>
> **fool·ish** / fōōl'ish / *adjective:* stupid; not wise: *It's **foolish** to go to work when you're sick.*
>
> **ar·gue** / ar'gyōō / *verb:* to fight with words; to disagree: *Michelle and Brendan **argue** a lot about politics. She's a Democrat and he's a Republican.*
>
> **ar·gu·ment** / ar'gyə-mənt / *noun:* a fight with words; a disagreement: *Shawn likes to save money, and his wife likes to spend it. This causes a lot of **arguments**.*
>
> **shout** / shout / *verb:* to say something in a very loud voice: *You don't have to **shout**. I can hear you.* —*noun:* a loud call: *We heard a **shout** in the hall and went to see what was happening.*
>
> **bit·ter** / bit'ər / *adjective* **1:** having a sharp, unpleasant taste: *I never chew aspirin. It tastes **bitter**.* **2:** having strong, angry feelings: *Larry and Brian had a **bitter** fight, and they're no longer friends.*

COMPLETING SENTENCES

Complete the sentences with these words. *Use each word twice. Where a word has different endings, both forms are given.*

argue/argument	bitter	fool/foolish	shout/shouts

1. The lemonade is _____. Put some sugar in it.

2. When our class gets noisy, the teacher _____ at us.

3. Just do what you're told and don't _____ with me.

4. We were _____ to buy a used car. We've had a lot of problems with it.

5. There was an accident in the parking lot, and the drivers got into a (an) _____ .

6. Today the United States and Japan are good friends, but in World War II they were _____ enemies.

7. I came quickly when I heard a _____ for help.

8. You would be a _____ to believe everything you read in that newspaper.

STORY COMPLETION

Discuss or think about these questions before completing the story that follows.

1. Why is work in a factory dull?

2. Why is the pay low?

3. Why do factories today need fewer workers?

Complete the story with these words.

| earn | bitter | shout | at least |
| dull | quit | argument | foolish |

Working in a Factory

Jerry works in a pencil factory, and his job is very _____ . He does the same thing every day. The factory is also dirty, and the machines make a lot of noise. If Jerry wants to talk to another worker, he has to _____ .

The biggest problem, however, is that Jerry's pay is low. Naturally, he wants to _____ more money.

Last month, Jerry and his boss had a long _____ about his salary. He told the boss that he never misses work and that his pay was too low. His boss promised to pay him more, but now he says it's impossible. Jerry is _____ about this. A promise is a promise, he says.

Jerry thinks it would be _____ to keep working in the factory. He's not going to get more money, and he doesn't trust his boss anymore. Tomorrow he's going to _____ and look for a job that pays _____ $10 an hour.

Discuss these questions and topics in pairs or small groups.

1. Why do people **quit** their jobs? Give as many reasons as you can.

2. Complete the following sentences. A. A new small car, for example, a Honda Civic, costs **at least** _____ dollars. B. I'm **at least** _____ feet _____ inches tall.

3. Some things we do are **dull** and some are interesting. Complete these sentences. _____ is dull. _____ is interesting.

4. In the area where you live, what do you think the average factory worker **earns** in a year? The average secretary? The average teacher? The average doctor?

5. Name some things that people do that are **foolish**, such as, driving too fast.

6. People **argue** about politics, sports, and many other things. Tell us something you argue about. Who do you argue with? Friends? Parents? Husband? Wife?

7. Why do parents **shout** at their children? Do you think it's a good way to get them to listen and do what they're told? Explain your answer.

8. Name as many things as you can that taste **bitter.**

Complete the sentences with these words. *If necessary, add an ending to the word so it forms a correct sentence.* (adj. = adjective and adv. = adverb)

1. **to earn** (verb)   **earnings** (noun)

    A. The government taxes our _____.

    B. Major league baseball players _____ a lot of money.

2. **to fool** (verb)   **foolish** (adj.)

    foolishly (adv.)   **foolishness** (noun)

    A. Someone took the packages we _____ left in our car.

    B. It's hard to _____ Stacy. She's very smart.

    C. Erin hasn't been feeling well, but she won't go to the doctor. What _____!

    D. Ernie had a lot to drink at the party. He was _____ to drive home.

3. **bitter** (adj.)   **bitterly** (adv.)   **bitterness** (noun)

   A. Terry cried _____ when her husband died.

   B. Our basketball team lost a big game by one point. It was a _____ loss.

   C. There was much _____ in the African-American community after the shooting of Martin Luther King, Jr.

BUILDING NOUNS WITH -NESS

The suffix **-ness** is added to adjectives to form a noun. For example, *weak + ness = weakness; kind + ness = kindness.*

-Ness *means the condition of being or the quality of being. Weakness means the condition of being weak; kindness means the quality of being kind.*

Adjective	Noun	Adjective	Noun
bitter	bitterness	happy	happiness
careless	carelessness	kind	kindness
dark	darkness	sad	sadness
foolish	foolishness	serious	seriousness
friendly	friendliness	sick	sickness
good	goodness	soft	softness
great	greatness	weak	weakness

Circle the letter next to the word that best completes the sentence.

   1. Does the president understand the _____ of the problem?

      a. sadness   c. seriousness

      b. darkness   d. sickness

   2. Sarah often eats too much. It's a _____ of hers.

      a. greatness   c. carelessness

      b. weakness   d. happiness

   3. Many people like Dennis because of his _____.

      a. softness   c. friendliness

      b. sadness   d. bitterness

4. Everyone is looking for _____.

    a. happiness   c. softness

    b. seriousness   d. greatness

5. We couldn't see the house because of the _____.

    a. carelessness   c. bitterness

    b. darkness   d. foolishness

6. I like the warmth and _____ of the blanket.

    a. greatness   c. friendliness

    b. seriousness   d. softness

7. It's easy to ask Elsie for help because of her _____.

    a. kindness   c. sadness

    b. happiness   d. foolishness

8. The fire was started by the _____ of a smoker.

    a. weakness   c. friendliness

    b. bitterness   d. carelessness

READING HELP-WANTED ADS

Tom wanted to quit school and go to work to earn money. That's why he read the Help-Wanted ads in the newspaper. Here are some of the ads and abbreviations he read.

Abbreviation	Meaning
1. exp. or exper.	experience; experienced
2. req.	required (necessary)
3. hr.—wk.—mo.	hour—week—month
4. P/T; F/T	part-time; full-time
5. M/F	male/female
6. excel. or exc.	excellent
7. bnfts.	benefits
8. neg.	negotiable
9. avail.	available
10. info.	information
11. HSD	high-school diploma

12.	GED	high-school equivalency diploma
13.	lic.	license
14.	ext.	extension

A.

> **Auto Mechanic**
>
> Exper. mechanic wanted. Must
> have driver's lic. Salary neg.
> Excel. bnfts. Call 212-823-3131.
> Ask for Max.

1. What two things do you need for this job?

2. What will your salary be?

3. What kind of benefits does the ad say you will get?

4. Who are you going to talk with about the job?

B.

> **Airline Now Hiring**
>
> Many entry-level positions.
> Top pay. 18 years or older.
> HSD/GED req. 1-800-441-6239

1. Do you need a college education for these jobs? How much education do you need?

2. How old must you be?

3. Do you need experience?

4. Who will pay for a phone call to ask about the jobs?

C.

> **Salad Chef M/F**
> Wash, peel, cut, and mix
> vegetables for potato and
> green salads. 3 mos. exp.,
> $8 per hr., 40 hrs. per wk.,
> 11 AM–8 PM with 1 hr. break.
> 201-472-9605

1. Is this job open to men and women? How do you know?
2. How much experience do you need?
3. How much do you earn per hour? Per week?
4. How many days a week do you work?
5. Do you get paid for your break?

D.

> **Waiters/Waitresses FT/PT**
> All shifts avail. Good pay & tips,
> excel. bnfts. Apply in person.
> Billy's Diner, 906 Valley Rd.,
> Paterson, N.J.

1. Are these full-time or part-time jobs? Or are both available?
2. What does the ad say about hours?
3. What does the ad say about benefits?
4. Why doesn't the ad give a phone number?
5. Which of the four jobs in the ads would you apply for? Why?

ACTIVITY

Look at the Help-Wanted ads in a newspaper. *Circle in red two or three jobs that interest you. Bring the ads into class. To find the Help-Wanted ads, look at the index of the newspaper. The index is usually on page 2. Then look under "Classified Ads."*

USING THE INTERNET TO FIND INFORMATION

1. *Enter* the keywords ***reasons to stay in school*** *in the search box of any general search engine such as Google or Yahoo. Click on the "search" button or hit "enter" on the keyboard. The search engine will lead you to a list of Web sites.*

   Click on the links to two or three of these Web sites. Look over these sites and choose the one that seems the most interesting and that tells you the most about reasons to stay in school. Read a page or two. (Option: write down two or three reasons to stay in school that you learned about from this site.)

2. *Enter* the keywords ***Thomas Edison biography*** *in the search box of any general search engine such as Google or Yahoo. Click on the "search" button or hit "enter" on the keyboard. The search engine will lead you to a list of Web sites.*

   Click on the links to two or three of these Web sites. Look over these sites and choose the one that seems the most interesting and that tells you the most about Thomas Edison. Read a page or two. (Option: write down two or three things you learned about Thomas Edison from this site.)

SYNONYMS

Next to each sentence, write the word that has the same meaning or almost the same meaning as the part of the sentence in bold print.

aims	average	shallow	foolish
earn	at least	dull	quit

1. _____ If we go by car, the trip will take **a minimum of** eight hours.

2. _____ The desk looks nice, but the drawers are **not deep**.

3. _____ On Friday we **stop** work an hour early.

4. _____ Heather **plans** to start her own business soon.

5. _____ The show was **not interesting**.

6. _____ I was **stupid** to listen to Nat. He didn't know what he was talking about.

7. _____ Bruce Springsteen isn't an **ordinary** singer. He's a superstar.

8. _____ Carpenters and plumbers **make** good money.

SENTENCE COMPLETION

Complete the sentences with these words.

hesitant	shouted	pool	shot
drag	bitter	dive	argue

1. My sister and I often _____ about sports.

2. The detective _____ the man in the leg.

3. Juana and Diego are buying a _____ for their backyard.

4. A tree fell across the road. It took three people to _____ it away.

5. The Cold War between the United States and the Soviet Union was long and _____.

6. I was _____ to borrow my friend's car.

7. It takes a lot of practice to learn to swim and _____ well.

8. When Adam saw that he was locked in the room, he _____ for help.

STORY COMPLETION

Complete the story with these words.

lift	prefers	huge	spends
stream	hunting	deep	edge

A Fisherman

Josh and his cousin Neil often go _____, but Neil _____ to fish. He _____ a lot of time fishing in a _____ a few miles from his house. He stands at the _____ of the water and waits for the fish to bite.

Neil also enjoys fishing in the ocean where the water, of course, is _____ and the fish are larger. One day when he was fishing in the ocean, Neil caught a _____ fish. It was so heavy that he needed help to _____ it out of the water. He was very proud of his big catch.

Newcomers from Columbia

A Struggle

PREVIEW QUESTIONS

Discuss or think about these questions before reading the story.

1. Why do most immigrants come to the United States? Why did you come?

2. How did you feel when you first came?

3. How much English did you know? Was that a big problem? Explain your answer.

A Struggle

Luis is from Medellín, the second largest city in Colombia. He loves Medellín, but he wasn't able to get a good job there. That's why he came to the United States ten years **ago.** He had a cousin in Philadelphia, and he shared an apartment with him for two years. Then he met and married Gloria, a pretty young girl from Medellín. They met at a dance in Philadelphia and soon fell in love.

Life in the United States has been a **struggle** for Luis. The first year was especially difficult. He missed his family and friends back in Medellín. He had only a few relatives in Philadelphia and no friends.

The weather was also a problem. He came to Philadelphia in January, and he **wasn't used to** the cold. It's never cold and it never snows in Medellín. During his second day in Philadelphia, there was a big **storm.** Twenty inches of snow fell in 30 hours. The snow was pretty, but Luis couldn't go anywhere for three days.

His biggest problem was to find a job. When he came to Philadelphia, he was only 20 and he didn't have many **skills.** But his cousin had a friend who worked at a **bakery** that needed help. Luis never **baked** before, but he learned by watching and working with another **baker.** He worked long hours baking bread, pies, and cake. It wasn't fun and he wasn't making much money, but at least he had a job and could pay his expenses.

English was another problem. Luis didn't speak any English and understood very little. Fortunately, the other baker spoke Spanish, but Luis knew that English was important. Since he worked nights and slept in the morning, he studied English three afternoons a week at Philadelphia Community College on Market Street. In the beginning he was afraid of making mistakes, but his teacher was understanding and he learned quickly.

Luis worked at the bakery for five years, but he wanted to make more money. He and another baker decided to quit and open their own bakery. "Of course it wasn't easy," he says. "We had to borrow money, hire workers, and rent a store. We didn't make any money for six months."

Now their business is doing very well. It's especially busy all day Saturday and on Sunday morning. Luis works hard and **accomplishes** a lot. He makes good money, saves some, and has a nice car. He also speaks English **quite** well and understands everything others say.

Answer these questions about the story. *Use your experience and own ideas to answer questions with an asterisk (*). Work in pairs or small groups. The numbers in parentheses show which paragraph in the story has the answer.*

1. Why did Luis come to the United States? (1)

2. Why was the weather a problem for him? (3)

3. What happened his second day in Philadelphia? (3)

4. Why was it difficult for him to find a job? (4)

*5. Do you think people often get jobs with the help of a friend? Explain your answer.

6. How did Luis learn how to bake? (4)

7. How much English did he speak and understand when he came to the United States? (5)

8. What did he do to learn English? (5)

*9. Do you think he spoke much English outside of class? Do you? Explain your answers.

*10. Do you think fear of making mistakes often keeps people from speaking English?

11. What did Luis and his friend decide to do? (6)

12. When is their bakery especially busy? (7)

Guess the meaning of the key words in these sentences. *Use the context of the story to help you. Circle your answers.*

1. Life in the United States has been **a struggle** for Luis.

   a. fun
   b. a mistake
   c. a waste of time
   d. hard work

2. He came to Philadelphia in January, and he **wasn't used to** the cold. It's never cold in Medellín.

   a. wasn't afraid of
   b. wasn't familiar with
   c. wasn't happy about
   d. wasn't thinking about

3. Luis works hard and **accomplishes** a lot.

   a. talks
   b. helps others
   c. hurries
   d. does

WORD ENTRIES

> **a·go** / ə-gō′ / *adjective:* before now; in the past: *Nancy lived in New York for many years, but she moved to California six months **ago**.*
>
> **strug·gle** / strug′əl / *noun:* hard work; great effort: *Learning English was a **struggle** for Mohammed.* —*verb:* to work hard to get or do something: *Dave is **struggling** to support his family.*
>
> **be used to** / bē yo͞os to͞o *or* bē yo͞os′tə / *idiom:* to be familiar with: *Lauren **is used to** helping sick people; she's a nurse.*
>
> **storm** / stôrm / *noun:* heavy rain or snow, often with a strong wind: *A **storm** is coming. We're going to get a lot of rain.*

COMPLETING SENTENCES

Complete the sentences with these words. *Use each word twice. Where a word has different endings, both forms are given.*

is used to/am used to	ago	storm	struggle/struggling

1. We ate lunch an hour _____.

2. Politics is a _____ for power.

3. I often work 12 hours a day. I _____ working long hours.

4. Close the windows before you leave. We may get a _____.

5. Jason is very tired, but he wants to finish his homework. He's _____ to stay awake.

6. If this _____ continues, we're staying home tonight.

7. Anna is a bus driver. She _____ driving in bad weather.

8. Our new sofa came three days _____.

WORD ENTRIES

> **skill** / skil / *noun:* the ability to do something well because of practice and training: *Reading and writing are basic **skills**.*
>
> **bake** / bāk / *verb:* to cook in an oven: *Jamie is **baking** cookies for the party.*
>
> **bak·er** / bā′kər / *noun:* a person who bakes: *Mary Anne is a **baker**. She's taking the bread out of the ovens.*
>
> **bak·er·y** / bāk′ə-rē *or* bāk′rē / *noun:* a store that sells cakes, pies, bread, cookies, etc.: *I'm going to the **bakery** to buy a birthday cake for my daughter.*
>
> **ac·com·plish** / ə-kom′plish / *verb:* to do something, especially something important; to finish: *We'll have to work hard to **accomplish** what we want to do.*
>
> **quite** / kwīt / *adverb:* very (but *very* is stronger than *quite*): *This room is **quite** warm. I'm going to open the window.*

COMPLETING SENTENCES

Complete the sentences with these words. *Use each word twice. Where a word has different endings, both forms are given.*

accomplish/accomplished	skill/skills	bake/baking	quite

1. Computer _____ are important in many jobs.

2. Stephanie is _____ tall.

3. Francisco talks a lot, but he doesn't _____ much.

4. Jennifer is _____ fish for dinner.

5. Don is very good at fixing cars. This _____ got him a job at a service station.

6. How long will it take to _____ the potatoes?

7. Tania is _____ intelligent. She should do well in school.

8. We _____ a lot at yesterday's meeting.

Discuss or think about these questions before completing the story that follows.

1. Why is going out for dinner a good way to celebrate a wedding anniversary?
2. Who usually takes care of young children when both parents work full-time?
3. Why is taking care of young children hard work?

Complete the story with these words.

skill	storm	accomplish	baked
quite	are used to	struggle	ago

Vinnie and Marge

Vinnie and Marge got married six years _____ yesterday. They were going to celebrate their anniversary by going out for dinner, but there was a big _____ yesterday. So much snow fell that they decided to stay home.

Vinnie cooked dinner, and Marge _____ a cake. Vinnie isn't a great cook, but the dinner tasted _____ good, and the cake was delicious.

Both Vinnie and Marge work full-time, and they have two young children. Working and taking care of two small children is often a _____. It takes a lot of time, patience, and _____.

During the week, Vinnie and Marge have almost no free time, so they shop, clean the house, and visit their friends and relatives on the weekends. They _____ a lot in two days. It's not easy, but they _____ it by now.

Discuss these questions and topics in pairs or small groups.

1. How long **ago** did you come to the United States?

2. People do things differently in different countries. **Are** you **used to** the way people do things in the United States? Are you used to the weather here?

3. Do you think that life is a **struggle** for everyone, including those who are rich?

4. There are many types of **storms,** for example, snowstorms, thunderstorms, and hurricanes. Describe a bad storm that you remember.

5. A **skill** is an ability to do something. Cooking, driving, and sewing are skills. Name a skill that you have and one that you don't by completing these sentences. I can _____. I can't _____.

6. In the past, people **baked** more than they do today. Why?

7. Tell us about something you have **accomplished** or that you are trying to accomplish.

8. Use the word **quite** to describe yourself or someone you know. For example, "I'm quite thin." "Frank is quite strong."

WORD FAMILIES

Complete the sentences with these words. *If necessary, add an ending to the word so it forms a correct sentence.* (adj. = adjective and adv. = adverb)

1. **storm** (noun)   **stormy** (adj.)

   A. We can't go out in the boat today. We're going to have a bad
      _____.

   B. Look at those clouds! It's going to be a _____ day.

2. **skill** (noun)   **skillful** (adj.)   **skillfully** (adv.)

   A. Ben is a _____ carpenter.

   B. A doctor needs a lot of _____.

   C. The lawyer presented her case _____.

3. **to accomplish** (verb)   **accomplishment** (noun)

   A. Winning a gold medal in the Olympic Games is a great _____.

   B. What do you hope to _____ today?

BUILDING NOUNS WITH -ION

The suffix **-ion** (**-tion**, **-ition**, **-ation**, **-sion**) is added to verbs to form a noun. For example, *protect + ion = protection; add + ition = addition.*

The suffix **-ion** usually means *the act of* or *the result of.* For example, *protection* means *the act or result of protecting; addition* means *the act or result of adding.*

Verb	Noun	Verb	Noun
act	action	explore	exploration
add	addition	hesitate	hesitation
decide	decision	move	motion
discuss	discussion	prepare	preparation
educate	education	pronounce	pronunciation
examine	examination	protect	protection
explain	explanation	separate	separation

Circle the letter next to the word that best completes the sentence.

1. The store owners asked the police for better _____.

   a. hesitation   c. education
   b. protection   d. exploration

2. Our group had an interesting _____ about marriage.

   a. action   c. pronunciation
   b. addition   d. discussion

3. The _____ of the ship made me seasick.

    a. motion   c. explanation

    b. preparation   d. separation

4. A good _____ will help you get a job.

    a. protection   c. education

    b. hesitation   d. addition

5. Your _____ of English is much better now.

    a. separation   c. decision

    b. addition   d. pronunciation

6. Our history _____ was long and difficult, but I think I did well.

    a. examination   c. hesitation

    b. protection   d. motion

7. It was very cold this morning, but my car started without _____.

    a. exploration   c. hesitation

    b. protection   d. discussion

8. We have to do more than just talk about the problem. We must take

_____.

    a. education   c. examination

    b. action   d. addition

1. *Enter* the keywords **facts, Colombia** *in the search box of any general search engine such as Google or Yahoo. Click on the "search" button or hit "enter" on the keyboard. The search engine will lead you to a list of Web sites.*

   Click on the links to two or three of these Web sites. Look over these sites and choose the one that seems the most interesting and that tells you the most about Colombia. Read a page or two. (Option: write down two or three things you learned about Colombia from this site.)

2. *Enter* the keywords **Community College of Philadelphia** *in the search box of any general search engine such as Google or Yahoo. Click on the "search" button or hit "enter" on the keyboard. The search engine will lead you to a list of Web sites.*

   Click on the links to two or three of these Web sites. Look over these sites and choose the one that seems the most interesting and that tells you the most about the Community College of Philadelphia. Read a page or two. (Option: write down two or three things you learned about the Community College of Philadelphia from this site.)

CHAPTER 11

A Dream

PREVIEW QUESTIONS

Discuss or think about these questions before reading the story.

1. Are you happy with the apartment you rent? Or the house you rent or own?

2. Why is it better to buy a house than to rent an apartment or house if a family has enough money?

3. Sometimes people buy a house that is in poor condition. Why do they do this?

A Dream

Luis and his wife, Gloria, live in a nice apartment, but it isn't big **enough.** The kitchen and the living room are small. There are only two bedrooms, and they need three. They have two sons, Carlos and Diego, and a daughter, Maria, and they want her to have her own room. She's seven and the boys are four and two. They also want to have a yard for the children to play in.

Their **dream** is to buy a house, and they have already looked at some houses online. One of them was beautiful and had a modern kitchen, central air-conditioning, and a big yard, but it was very expensive. Luis and Gloria don't have enough money to buy it. The bakery is their only income, and it isn't making enough money for them to buy an expensive house. That's why they're **seaching** for one that doesn't cost a lot, and, of course, that's almost impossible to find.

Yesterday a real estate agent showed them four houses, and three of them were great. They didn't need painting and were in good **repair,** and one of them had a pool. But it was the same story. They couldn't afford the houses they liked, and they didn't like the house they could afford.

The affordable one was old and had **cracks** in the walls. The owner didn't take good care of it. Now he has to move to Chicago to take a new job, and he's in a hurry to sell. The house needs painting and many repairs, but it has one **advantage**—it costs $70,000 to $90,000 less than the other three houses.

Last night, Luis and Gloria talked about the old house for two hours. "I know we won't find anything that costs less, and I want to move as soon as I can," said Luis. "And I'm tired of looking at houses we can't afford," Gloria said. **So** they decided to buy the old house and repair it.

The house will **require** a lot of work, but it's in a nice neighborhood and the backyard is big. It will look beautiful when they're finished with it. Luis and Gloria are good at painting, and some of their friends will help with the repairs. The children will be happy to have their own house where they can make all the noise they want, and Maria will be happy to have her own room. Tomorrow Luis and Gloria are going to a bank to ask for a loan.

TRUE OR FALSE

If the sentence is true, write *T*. If it's false, write *F*.

_____ 1. Luis and Gloria have a large apartment.

_____ 2. They want Maria to have her own room.

_____ 3. They have already looked at some houses online, and one was very nice.

_____ 4. They can easily find a house they can afford.

_____ 5. They didn't like any of the houses they looked at yesterday.

_____ 6. The house they can afford needs painting and many repairs.

_____ 7. Luis wants to move, but he's in no hurry.

_____ 8. Luis and Gloria plan to do a lot of their own work on the house.

WHAT DO YOU THINK?

Use your experience, judgment, and the story to answer these questions.

1. The cost of a house depends on many things, for example, its location. What else does its cost depend on?

2. Luis and Gloria are going to paint and repair their home with the help of some friends. Will that save them a lot of money? Explain your answer.

3. Why can't the children make all the noise they want in their apartment?

4. What questions will they ask Luis and Gloria at the bank?

WORD GUESSING

Guess the meaning of the key words in these sentences. *Use the context of the story to help you. Circle your answers.*

1. **Their dream is to** buy a house, and they have already looked at some that are for sale.

   a. they think it's easy to

   b. they want very much to

   c. they know they can

   d. they know they can't

2. That's why Luis and Gloria are **searching for** a house that doesn't cost a lot, and, of course, that's not easy to find.

    a. buying   c. looking for

    b. hoping for   d. thinking of

3. **So** Luis and Gloria decided to buy the old house and repair it.

    a. that's why   c. later

    b. but   d. however

MINI-DICTIONARY—PART ONE

WORD ENTRIES

e·nough / i-nuf′ / *adjective:* as much or as many as needed; sufficient: *Do we have* **enough** *time to stop and visit our friends?* —*adverb:* to the amount or degree necessary: *My car is big* **enough*** *for five people.*
*When **enough** is used as an adverb, it is placed after the adjective or adverb it goes with.

dream / drēm / *noun* **1:** images the mind sees in sleep: *I went to sleep and had a* **dream** *that I was the president of the United States.* **2:** something one wants very much, but that is difficult or impossible to get: *José's* **dream** *is to graduate from college and get a good job.* —*verb**: to have a dream: *Last night Wayne* **dreamt** *he won a million dollars in the lottery.*
*The past tense of **dream** is **dreamed** or **dreamt**.

search / sûrch / *verb:* to look carefully for something: *Nick is* **searching** *everywhere for his ring.* —*noun:* the act of looking carefully for something: *In 1849 many people rushed to California in* **search** *of gold.*

crack / krak / *noun:* a small break or separation in a wall, cup, etc.: *There's a* **crack** *in the mirror.* —*verb:* to cause a small separation in a cup, dish, etc.: *The water was so hot that it* **cracked** *a dish.*

COMPLETING SENTENCES

Complete the sentences with these words. *Use each word twice. Where a word has different endings, both forms are given.*

search/searching	enough	crack/cracked	dream/dreamt

1. The engineers are checking the _____ in the bridge.

2. Grace is _____ for a job.

3. I don't know what it means, but I _____ about you last night.

4. That's _____ spaghetti. I can't eat any more.

5. After a long _____, my husband found his keys.

6. I dropped the glass and it _____.

7. Gene wasn't fast _____ to win the race.

8. Manuela's _____ is to be a doctor.

MINI-DICTIONARY—PART TWO

WORD ENTRIES

re·pair / ri-pâr′ / *verb:* to fix something; to put something back in good condition: *They're going to **repair** the road in the spring. —noun*:* the act or result of repairing: *I have to bring my car to a service station for **repairs**.*
***Repair** is often used in the plural form.

ad·van·tage / ad-van′tij / *noun:* something that helps a person; something that make a thing better: *A good education is a big **advantage** in life.*

so / sō / *adverb:* that is why; for that reason*: *We were hungry, **so** we stopped to eat.*
***So** has other meanings. It often means *very: Everyone likes Tina. She's **so** nice.*

re·quire / ri-kwīr′ / *verb:* to need; to say something is necessary; to order: *Dogs are great pets, but they **require** a lot of care.*

COMPLETING SENTENCES

Complete the sentences with these words. *Use each word twice. Where a word has different endings, both forms are given.*

repair/repaired	so	advantage/advantages	require/requires

1. The restaurant we're going to _____ men to wear jackets.
2. Jan had a toothache, _____ he went to the dentist.
3. When my toilet broke, I called a plumber to _____ it.
4. The _____ of leaving early is that traffic will be light.
5. Most babies _____ ten or eleven hours of sleep a night.
6. The eye doctor _____ Jim's glasses.
7. Having money isn't everything, but it has its _____.
8. The suit was very expensive, _____ I didn't buy it.

STORY COMPLETION

Discuss or think about these questions before completing the story that follows.

1. Do you dream much? Can you remember a dream you had recently?
2. A dream in which something very bad happens is called a nightmare. Do you ever have nightmares?
3. Do you believe in dreams—do you think that what you see in a dream is likely to happen in real life?

Complete the story with these words.

advantages	enough	searching	so
repair	dreamt	require	cracks

The Old School Bus

Jack is a mechanic who works for a public school system in Texas. One of his jobs is to check the school buses and keep them in good condition. Last night he _____ that someone stole an old school bus from the high school and that everyone was _____ for it.

When Jack got to work this morning, the first thing he did was to check the old bus. The motor didn't sound right, the bus needed new brakes, and a window had some _____ in it. Jack feels the bus isn't safe _____ for the students, _____ he's writing a report for the high school principal and the board of education.

The report says it's possible to _____ the bus, but it'll _____ a lot of work, and that'll be expensive. It would be better to buy a new one.

There are many _____ to a new bus. It'll be bigger, cleaner, and much safer. It'll be less expensive to maintain. As soon as he finishes the report, Jack is going to give it to Mrs. Johnson, the high-school principal.

SHARING INFORMATION

Discuss these questions and topics in pairs or small groups.

1. Do you have **enough** space in the apartment or house in which you live? For example, are the kitchen and the closets big enough?

2. We all have **dreams**—hopes for the future. Complete this sentence. My dream is to

   _____.

3. The Internet is a good place to **search** for information. How do you search for information on the net? Do you often use the Internet to get information?

4. We see **cracks** in many things, such as windows. Name some other things in which we sometimes see cracks.

5. When a person is good at making small **repairs**, we say that person is handy—good with his or her hands. Are you handy?

6. Many people leave their family, friends, and country to live in the United States. What are some of the **advantages** of living in the United States? What are some **disadvantages?**

7. Complete this sentence. Ernie has a headache and fever, **so** he _____

   _____.

8. Our bodies **require** rest. Name four other things our bodies require.

   a. _____   c. _____
   b. _____   d. _____

WORD FAMILIES

Complete the sentences with these words. *If necessary, add an ending to the word so it forms a correct sentence.* (adj. = adjective and adv. = adverb)

1. **advantage** (noun)   **advantageous** (adj.)   **disadvantage** (noun)

   A. Roger is going to college in September. He doesn't know much about computers. That's a (an) _____ .

   B. Fortunately, our army was in a (an) _____ position when the enemy attacked.

   C. Caroline is very tall. That's a (an) _____ when she plays basketball.

2. **to require** (verb)   **requirement** (noun)

   A. That's a bad cut! It's going to _____ stitches.

   B. A high-school education is a _____ for many jobs.

BUILDING WORDS WITH *DIS-*

The prefix **dis-** is placed before nouns, adjectives, and verbs to form a new word. For example, *dis + honest = dishonest; dis + advantage = disadvantage.*

The prefix **dis-** means *not* or *the opposite of.* For example, *dishonest* means *not honest; disadvantage* is *the opposite of advantage.*

Original Word	New Word	Original Word	New Word
advantage	disadvantage	obey	disobey
agree	disagree	order	disorder
appear	disappear	please	displease
continue	discontinue	repair	disrepair
courage	discourage	respect	disrespect
honest	dishonest	satisfied	dissatisfied
like	dislike		

Circle the letter next to the word that best completes the sentence.

1. If we don't pay our phone bill soon, they'll _____ our service.

   a. disobey   c. discontinue

   b. discourage   d. dislike

2. Courtney doesn't like her teacher, but she never shows any _____.

    a. disrespect   c. disadvantage

    b. disrepair   d. disorder

3. We don't trust George. We think he's _____.

    a. discouraged   c. dissatisfied

    b. dishonest   d. displeased

4. What's a _____ of living in a big city?

    a. disadvantage   c. dislike

    b. disrepair   d. disorder

5. I'm going to another dentist. I _____ the one I have.

    a. discourage   c. displease

    b. disobey   d. dislike

6. If there is any more _____ at this party, I'm calling the police.

    a. disrespect   c. disorder

    b. disrepair   d. disadvantage

7. My wallet _____. I can't find it anywhere.

    a. disobeyed   c. disliked

    b. disagreed   d. disappeared

8. After many years of _____, it's going to be difficult to fix the building.

    a. disadvantages   c. disorder

    b. disrepair   d. disrespect

USING THE INTERNET TO FIND INFORMATION

1. *Enter* the keywords **real estate agents, U.S. Department of Labor** *in the search box of any general search engine such as Google or Yahoo. Click on the "search" button or hit "enter" on the keyboard. The search engine will lead you to a list of Web sites.*

   Click on the links to two or three of these Web sites. Look over these sites and choose the one that seems the most interesting and that tells you the most about real estate agents. Read a page or two. (Option: write down two or three things you learned about real estate agents from this site.)

2. *Enter* the keywords **the price of houses in the U.S.** *in the search box of any general search engine such as Google or Yahoo. Click on the "search" button or hit "enter" on the keyboard. The search engine will lead you to a list of Web sites.*

   Click on the links to two or three of these Web sites. Look over these sites and choose the one that seems the most interesting and that tells you the most about the price of houses in the U.S. Read a page or two. (Option: write down two or three things you learned about the price of houses from this site.)

CHAPTER 12

A Visit

PREVIEW QUESTIONS

Discuss or think about these questions before reading the story.

1. Do you visit friends or relatives often? How often?

2. Do you fall asleep easily?

3. Have you ever fallen asleep when visiting friends?

A Visit

Saturday is always Luis' busiest day at the bakery, but last Saturday was busier than most. One of his bakers was sick, and that meant more work for Luis. When he came home from work, he was **weary**. He hoped to stay home, watch a little TV, and go to bed early. He forgot that Gloria wanted to visit some of their friends from Medellín, Colombia. She had told her friends that they were coming so they couldn't stay home.

When Gloria and Luis arrived at their friends' house, he knew it was going to be difficult not to **fall asleep.** He falls asleep easily. Every night he watches the ten o'clock news, and every night he's asleep before the news is over. So he was happy when his friend offered him a cup of coffee. "I hope it's Colombian," he joked. "Of course it is—that's the only kind we serve," his friend replied with a smile. Luis drank two cups of black coffee, but he could **hardly** keep his eyes open.

Luis and Gloria were sitting in the living room, and he was OK **while** their friends were showing them photos. But when everyone started talking about the good old days in Medellín, he fell asleep. Gloria was next to him on the sofa. She **pinched** his arm, but it didn't help. She pinched him again. This time he **woke up.**

Luis drank another cup of coffee, and his friend opened a window for him. Luis was fine for a while, but then he fell asleep again and began to snore. When Luis snores, he makes a lot of noise.

Gloria was **ashamed** of Luis' snoring, and she was angry at him. Their friends came to the United States three months ago, and this was the first time they had visited them. However, his snoring didn't **disturb** them. They smiled and told Gloria to let him sleep. They know how hard he works.

On their way home, Gloria and Luis had an argument. She was still angry about his sleeping. "I think you should try harder to stay awake when we're visiting friends," she remarked. "And I think you should know enough not to ask me to visit friends on Saturday nights," he replied. "You know how tired I am after work on Saturday." Then he said he was sorry that he fell asleep and snored. She gave him a kiss and everything was OK.

Answer these questions about the story. *Use your experience and own ideas to answer questions with an asterisk. Work in pairs or small groups. The numbers in parentheses tell you which paragraph has the answer.*

1. Why was last Saturday busier than most for Luis? (1)

2. What did he hope to do when he came home from work? (1)

*3. Do you think Gloria should have called their friends and said they couldn't visit them that night because Luis was too tired? Explain your answer.

4. What happens to Luis when he watches the ten o'clock news? (2)

*5. Why does coffee keep people awake? Does it keep you awake?

6. When did Luis fall asleep? (3)

7. What did Gloria do when he fell asleep? (3)

8. What did he do after he fell asleep again? (4)

9. How did Luis' snoring make Gloria feel? (5)

10. How did their friends feel about his snoring? (5)

*11. Do you think this was the first time Luis fell asleep while visiting friends? Or do you think it happened before? Explain your answer.

12. What did Luis say that ended their argument? (6)

GUESSING FROM CONTEXT

Guess the meaning of the key words in these sentences. *Use the context of the story to help you. Circle your answers.*

1. When Luis came home from work, he was **weary.**

   a. hungry   c. happy
   b. tired   d. thirsty

2. Gloria **was ashamed of** Luis' snoring.

   a. was sad about   c. was quiet about
   b. was angry about   d. felt bad about

3. However, his snoring didn't **disturb their friends.**

   a. make them laugh   c. make them unhappy
   b. make them say anything d. make them think badly of him

WORD ENTRIES

> **wear·y** / wir′ē / *adjective:* very tired: *The basketball team has been practicing for three hours, and the players are **weary.***
>
> **fall a·sleep** / fôl ə-slēp′ / *idiom:* to begin to sleep: *Leo went to bed and immediately **fell asleep**. He was tired.*
> The past tense of **fall** is **fell**.
>
> **hard·ly** / härd′lē / *adverb:* only a little; with difficulty: *Speak louder, please. We can **hardly** hear you.*
>
> **while** / wīl or hwīl / *conjunction:* during the time that: *I read a magazine **while** I was waiting for the dentist.* —*noun:* an indefinite period of time, usually short: *Dinner will be ready in a little **while**.*

COMPLETING SENTENCES

Complete the sentences with these words. *Use each word twice. Where a word has different endings, both forms are given.*

hardly	weary	while	falls asleep/fell asleep

1. _____ you were watching TV, I was doing the dishes.

2. It's _____ raining now. I'm not going to wear a raincoat.

3. When Gary comes home from work, he sits down in his favorite chair and _____.

4. The battle lasted for three days, and the soldiers are _____.

5. The meeting was long and the room was hot. That's why I _____.

6. Take a break and rest a _____.

7. My neighbor wanted to borrow my car, but I didn't let him. I _____ know him.

8. By the end of the day we were _____.

WORD ENTRIES

---

pinch / pinch / *verb:* to press hard between the thumb and another finger: *The baby likes to* **pinch** *his mother's neck.* —*noun* **1**: the act of pinching: *That* **pinch** *hurt.* **2**: a very small amount: *The soup needs a* **pinch** *of salt.*

wake up / wāk up / *verb** **1**: to stop sleeping: *I usually* **wake up** *at six o'clock.* **2**: to make someone stop sleeping: *The alarm clock* **woke up** *Fred.*
The past tense of* **wake up *is* **woke up**.

shame / shām / *noun:* a painful feeling that comes from doing something wrong or foolish: *The boy's face turned red with* **shame** *when the teacher asked him if he cheated.*

a·shamed / ə-shāmd′ / *adjective:* feeling shame: *I'm* **ashamed** *of getting drunk at the party.*

dis·turb / dis-tûrb′ / *verb:* to upset someone; to break in on a person who is busy: *Please turn down the music. I'm trying to study, and it's* **disturbing** *me.*

COMPLETING SENTENCES

Complete the sentences with these words. *Use each word twice. Where a word has different endings, both forms are given.*

wake up/woke up	ashamed	disturb/disturbing	pinch/pinched

1. You should be _____ of stealing the radio from the store.
2. Bobby didn't like it when I _____ his side.
3. _____! It's late! You have to go to work!
4. Nicole is talking on her cell phone. Don't _____ her!
5. Jonathan added a _____ of salt to the mashed potatoes.
6. Karen felt _____ that she forgot her father's birthday.
7. The company's decision to close the factory is _____.
8. Tim _____ at 7:30.

Discuss or think about these questions before completing the story that follows.

1. How many of your classes are dull? Most of them? Some? One? None?

2. Did (do) you ever fall asleep in class? If so, why?

3. If a student frequently falls asleep in class, do you think the teacher should give the student a lower mark? Explain your answer.

Complete the story with these words.

disturbs	pinch	hardly	falls asleep
weary	while	wakes	ashamed

A Dull Teacher

Cindy works during the day and goes to college at night. Most of her classes are interesting, but her English teacher is dull. He never changes his tone of voice and the students call him "Mr. Monotone."

At the beginning of class, Cindy is fine, but after a _____ she feels tired, and sometimes she _____. The teacher doesn't say anything, but he sees her sleeping and it really _____ him. He tries to make his class interesting, but it never is.

Cindy isn't _____ of going to sleep in class, but she is afraid of getting a poor mark. She wants at least a B. So she has asked a friend who sits behind her to _____ her when she goes to sleep. This _____ her up, but Cindy is still so _____ that she can _____ stay awake.

Discuss these questions and topics in pairs or small groups.

1. Long physical or mental activity often makes us **weary**. Complete this sentence. After I _____ for a long time, I feel weary.

2. Do you ever **fall asleep** while watching TV?

3. Think of something you can do, but almost can't do. For example, "I can **hardly** swim." Then complete this sentence. I can hardly _____ _____.

4. A **while** is an indefinite period of time. It is usually a short period, but it can also be a long period of time. Name something that you haven't done in a long while. Or name someone you haven't seen in a long while.

5. Sometimes people give a child a little **pinch** on the cheek to express their affection. Do you think children like this? Did you when you were a child?

6. What time do you usually **wake up** in the morning? Who or what wakes you up?

7. Sometimes we feel **ashamed** when we shouldn't, but there are times when people should feel ashamed. Complete this sentence. I think people should feel ashamed when they _____.

8. Give an example of something or somebody that **disturbs** you.

WORD FAMILIES

Complete the sentences with these words. *If necessary, add an ending to the word so it forms a correct sentence.* (adj. = adjective and adv. = adverb)

1. **fall asleep** (idiom)   **asleep** (adj.)

   A. After I go to bed, it's a while before I _____.

   B. The children are in bed, but they aren't _____. I hear them talking.

2. **wake up** (idiom)   **awake** (adj.)

   A. It's 1:00 in the morning, but Phil is still _____. He's reading.

   B. Shh. Talk quietly. Don't _____ the baby.

3. **to disturb** (verb)   **disturbance** (noun)

   A. It _____ teachers when students talk a lot.

   B. There was a _____ at the dance, but it wasn't serious.

BUILDING NOUNS WITH -ANCE OR -ENCE

The suffix *-ance* or *-ence* is added to verbs and adjectives to form a noun. For example, *clear + ance = clearance, differ + ence = difference*. Words that already end in *-ant* or *-ent* drop the final *t* and add only *ce*. For example, *intelligent* drops its final *t* and adds *ce* to form *intelligence*.

When *-ance* or *-ence* is added to a verb, it means *the act of*. For example, *acceptance* means *the act of accepting*.

When *-ance* or *-ence* is added to an adjective, it means *the quality of being*. For example, *intelligence* means *the quality of being intelligent*.

Verb or Adjective	Noun	Verb or Adjective	Noun
accept	acceptance	excellent	excellence
appear	appearance	important	importance
assist	assistance	independent	independence
clear	clearance	intelligent	intelligence
different	difference	obedient	obedience
disturb	disturbance	silent	silence
enter	entrance		

Circle the letter next to the word that best completes the sentence.

1. The United States celebrates its _____ on July 4th.

   a. importance   c. acceptance
   b. independence   d. difference

2. We need a lawyer with a lot of skill and _____.

   a. clearance   c. obedience
   b. silence   d. intelligence

3. Everyone knows the _____ of good health.

   a. importance   c. entrance
   b. difference   d. acceptance

4. Selina is waiting for a letter of _____ from college.

    a. appearance   c. acceptance

    b. excellence   d. independence

5. There's a big _____ between the weather in New York and in Florida.

    a. disturbance   c. assistance

    b. clearance   d. difference

6. They're having a (an) _____ sale at the furniture store.

    a. acceptance   c. clearance

    b. entrance   d. appearance

7. Thanks a lot for your _____ at the party.

    a. assistance   c. obedience

    b. difference   d. importance

8. In the army, _____ is very important. You must follow orders.

    a. appearance   c. independence

    b. obedience   d. clearance

USING THE INTERNET TO FIND INFORMATION

1. *Enter* the keyword **Colombian coffee** *in the search box of any general search engine such as Google or Yahoo. Click on the "search" button or hit "enter" on the keyboard. The search engine will lead you to a list of Web sites.*

   Click on the links to two or three of these Web sites. Look over these sites and choose the one that seems the most interesting and that tells you the most about Colombian coffee. Read a page or two. (Option: write down two or three things you learned about Colombian coffee from this site.)

2. *Enter* the keyword **snoring** *in the search box of any general search engine such as Google or Yahoo. Click on the "search" button or hit "enter" on the keyboard. The search engine will lead you to a list of Web sites.*

   Click on the links to two or three of these Web sites. Look over these sites and choose the one that seems the most interesting and that tells you the most about snoring. Read a page or two. (Option: write down two or three things you learned about snoring from this site.)

LOOKING FOR AN APARTMENT AND A HOUSE

Luis and Gloria rented an apartment after they got married. Some years later they bought a house. In looking for an apartment and later for a house, they read many newspaper ads like the ones on pages 132 and 133. Ads A and B are rentals. C and D are houses for sale.

Abbreviation	Meaning	Abbreviation	Meaning
1. apt.	apartment	11. lg. or lrg.	large
2. avail. immed.	available immediately	12. LR	living room
		13. mod. kit.	modern kitchen
3. bath. or bth.	bathroom	14. move-in cond.	move-in condition
4. betwn.	between		
5. BR	bedroom	15. schls.	schools
6. DR	dining room	16. shpg.	shopping
7. fin. bsmnt.	finished basement	17. transp.	transportation
		18. w/	with
8. FP or fplc.	fireplace	19. w/w crptg.	wall-to-wall carpeting
9. gar.	garage		
10. H/HW incl.	heat/hot water included	20. yrd.	yard

A.
> beautiful 2 BR apt., mod.
> kit. and bath., lg. LR, H/HW incl.
> avail. immed., $1,200/mo.
> call 215-555-1872

1. How many bedrooms does this apartment have?
2. What does the ad say about the kitchen and bathroom?
3. Do you have to pay extra for heat and hot water?
4. When will you be able to rent the apartment?
5. How much rent will you have to pay?

B.

> 1 & 2 BR apts. avail., new
> kit. and bth., new w/w crptg.,
> h/hw incl., near transp.,
> no pets, call betwn. 9 AM &
> 9 PM, ask for Maria.
> 267-555-4591

1. What does the ad say about the kitchens and bathrooms?

2. What type of carpeting do the apartments have?

3. Can you keep a dog in these apartments?

4. Why are these apartments good for someone who doesn't own a car?

5. How can you find out how much the apartments rent for?

C.

> 4 lg. BRs, DR, 2 bths.,
> mod. kit., 2 car gar.,
> near schls. & shpg.,
> $150,000.
> 415-555-4242

1. What does the ad say about the bedrooms in this house?

2. How many bathrooms does it have?

3. What's good about the location of the house?

4. What's special about the garage?

5. How much does it cost?

D.

> By owner, LR w/fplc., DR, mod.
> eat-in kit., 3 BRs, 1 1/2
> bths., fin. bsmnt., lrg.
> yard. $230,000.
> 215-555-9368

1. What's special about the living room in this house?
2. What does the ad say about the kitchen?
3. How many bathrooms are there?
4. What kind of basement does the house have?
5. How does the ad describe the yard?

Which of the houses (C or D) do you like best? Explain your answer.

ACTIVITY

Look at the apartments for rent and houses for sale in the classified section of a newspaper. *Circle in red an apartment for rent and a house for sale, and bring the ads into class.*

SYNONYMS

Next to each sentence, write the word that has the same meaning or almost the same meaning as the part of the sentence in bold print.

baking	storm	accomplish	weary
required	while	searching	so

1. _____ Tony has two jobs. When he finishes the second, he's **very tired.**

2. _____ We're going to get a **lot of wind and rain** tonight.

3. _____ Yoko is **looking** for the money she lost.

4. _____ The bank **needed** more information before they would give me a loan.

5. _____ It was cloudy and cool on Saturday. **That's why** we didn't go to the beach.

6. _____ Steve is **cooking** the beans **in the oven.**

7. _____ I'm tired. I want to rest for a **short time.**

8. _____ Beth and I hope to **do** a lot tomorrow.

SENTENCE COMPLETION

Complete the sentences with these words.

advantage	disturbs	wake up	crack
fell asleep	skill	ashamed	pinched

1. I have to _____ the children soon, or they'll be late for school.

2. Both Greg and Alexi are good carpenters, but Greg has more experience and _____ .

3. I _____ myself to keep from laughing at my friend's mistake.

4. Marilyn speaks French well; that will give her a (an) _____ when she visits Paris.

5. Marissa is _____ of lying to her parents.

6. There is a _____ in the lamp. It fell on the floor.

7. It _____ Jenny when her neighbors have noisy parties.

8. Hank _____ while driving, and his car went off the road. Fortunately, he wasn't hurt.

Complete the story with these words.

repairing	while	ago	dream	enough
quite	struggle	hardly	was used to	

A Hard Worker

Andrew was born 30 years _____ in eastern Poland. He was the oldest of three children, and his father was a coal miner. His father worked hard but was paid very little. The family was _____ poor.

Andrew's _____ was to live in the United States. He could _____ speak English, but he was very good at _____ cars and he _____ hard work.

Andrew was very happy when he got his visa and left for the United States. However, finding a job in the United States was a _____. The biggest problem was that he didn't know _____ English. He worked in a factory _____ looking for a job as an auto mechanic. After a few months, he got a job as a mechanic at a service station, and he's doing very well now.

Newcomers from Italy

CHAPTER 13

Soccer Fans

PREVIEW QUESTIONS

Discuss or think about these questions before reading the story.

1. Do you like soccer?* Is it your favorite sport?

2. Do you play soccer? Do you watch it on TV? A lot?

3. Name some countries where soccer is a very popular sport.

4. Soccer is the most popular sport in the world. Why?

---

* In many countries soccer is called *futbol*. American football is a very different game.

Soccer Fans

Mario lives in Chicago, but he was born in Italy. He's a barber, and he's married and has two children, Sal and Marie. His wife, Connie, was born in the United States, but her parents are from Italy. She stays home and takes care of the children, but she plans to go to work when the children are older. She's more modern than Mario.

Mario and Connie are big soccer **fans.** But when Mario came to the United States eight years ago, he didn't know that soccer was a popular sport here. The only American sports that he heard a lot about were basketball, baseball, and football. He was **amazed** to learn that there were many soccer teams in the United States.

One Sunday afternoon, he was taking a walk and **discovered** two teams playing soccer in a park near his house. He watched the game. Both teams had excellent players, and the game was **exciting.** After the game, he talked to some of the players. They were from Italy, Latin America, and Spain. One of the teams needed another player, and they asked Mario to **join** their team. He was happy to join. Seven years later, he's still playing on the team, and he's one of their best players.

His son, Sal, goes to all of his dad's games and is also learning how to play soccer. Mario practices with him and shows him how to kick and pass the ball. He's only six years old, but he's fast and can kick and pass well. His ability to play soccer is amazing. "Like father, like son," their friends say. And Sal says, "I can't wait until I'm old enough to play on the school team."

Last week, Mario, Connie, and their two kids drove all the way from Chicago to Connecticut to visit Connie's cousins. It took them two days. She hadn't seen her cousins in five years, but the biggest reason for the trip was that her youngest cousin was getting married. She didn't want to miss the big wedding and the family reunion.

Connie's cousins are also crazy about soccer. One night her cousin Lou was playing soccer. It was the final game of the season, and the entire family went to the game. There was a large **crowd.** Mario and Connie **cheered** when Lou's team played well. The **score** was two to two at halftime. It was exciting. No one **scored** in the third quarter. Then, with only 60 seconds left in the game, Lou scored, and his team won three to two. After the game, they went to have pizza and to celebrate.

Answer these questions about the story. *Use your experience and own ideas to answer questions with an asterisk (*). Work in pairs or small groups. The numbers in parentheses tell you which paragraph in the story has the answer.*

   1. What does Mario do? And Connie? (1)

*2. Why do you think she's more modern than Mario?

   3. What were the only American sports that he heard a lot about? (2)

*4. Why isn't soccer more popular in the United States?

   5. What did Mario discover? (3)

   6. What did he do after the game? (3)

*7. Do you think Mario is proud of Sal? Explain your answer.

   8. Why doesn't Sal play soccer for his school team? (4)

   9. What did Mario, Connie, and the kids do last week? (5)

 10. What was the biggest reason for their trip? (5)

 11. What did they do when Lou's team played well? (6)

 12. What did Lou do with 60 seconds left in the game? (6)

GUESSING FROM CONTEXT

Guess the meaning of the key words in these sentences. *Use the context of the story to help you. Circle your answers.*

   1. Mario and Connie **are big soccer fans.**

      a. play a lot of soccer   c. coach a soccer team

      b. watch soccer on TV   d. are very interested in soccer

   2. Mario was **amazed** to learn that there were many soccer teams in the United States.

      a. glad   c. quick

      b. surprised   d. slow

   3. Both teams had excellent players, and the game was **exciting.**

      a. long   c. very interesting

      b. close   d. dull

WORD ENTRIES

fan / fan / *noun* **1**: someone who is very interested in a sport or a famous person: *Dick is a big basketball* **fan**. *He goes to a lot of games and watches them on TV.* **2**: an instrument that cools a room or area by making air move. *In the summer we put a* **fan** *in our living room.*

a·maze / ə-māze' / *verb*: to surprise very much: *Victor* **amazed** *his teacher by getting 100 on his test.*

dis·cov·er / dis-kuv'ər / *verb*: to find or to learn about something not known before: *Many people rushed to California in 1849 after someone* **discovered** *gold.*

ex·cit·ing / ik-sī'ting / *adjective*: causing strong feelings: *The book was so* **exciting** *that I couldn't put it down.*

COMPLETING SENTENCES

Complete the sentences with these words. *Use each word twice. Where a word has different endings, both forms are given.*

fan	discover/discovered	exciting	amazes/amazed

1. Everyone liked the movie. It was _____.

2. My daughter is a tennis _____.

3. The astronauts _____ the world when they landed on the moon.

4. I was angry when I _____ that someone took my money.

5. Carol is a _____ of Bruce Springsteen. She loves to hear him sing.

6. Our trip to Africa was _____.

7. Doctors are trying to _____ a cure for cancer.

8. The little boy plays the piano very well. He _____ me.

WORD ENTRIES

> **join** / join / *verb* **1**: to become a member of a group: *Lisa is going to **join** the army next week.* **2**: to do something with someone: *We're going to the park. Do you want to **join** us?*
>
> **crowd** / kroud / *noun*: a large number of people in one place: *The police are having trouble controlling the **crowd.***
>
> **cheer** / chēr / *verb*: to shout for a team or person: *The president is going by in his limousine and everyone is **cheering**. —noun*: shouting for a team or person: *A **cheer** went up from the fans when our team won the game.*
>
> **score** / skôr / *verb*: to make one or more points in a game: *Wayne is a terrific basketball player. He **scored** 30 points last night. —noun*: the number of points each team has in a game; the number of points a person receives on a test: *Our baseball team is winning by a **score** of 5 to 1.*

COMPLETING SENTENCES

Complete the sentences with these words. *Use each word twice. Where a word has different endings, both forms are given.*

crowd	score/scored	join	cheers/cheered

1. The students _____ when the teacher said there would be no school tomorrow.

2. It was a rainy day, so the _____ at the parade was small.

3. Come in and _____ the party.

4. Our football team _____ 21 points; the other team had only seven.

5. The _____ were so loud we could hear them outside the gym.

6. I'm going to _____ the Spanish Club at school.

7. Kunio got a high _____ on his test.

8. The _____ is waiting for the theater to open.

Discuss or think about these questions before completing the story that follows.

1. Do you like American football? Do you understand the game?
2. Did you ever go to a football game? Was it exciting?
3. Do you ever watch football on TV? How often?

Complete the story with these words.

cheered	scored	fan	discovered
joined	exciting	crowd	amazed

A Football Star

My name is Doug Brown and I go to Lincoln High School. I'm a good student and a sports _____. I especially like football. Every Sunday afternoon, I watch professional football on TV. The New York Giants are my favorite team.

I also like to play football, and I _____ our high-school team at the beginning of September. The coach and the team soon _____ that I was very fast, and now I play in every game.

On Saturday we played an important game against Washington High School. They hadn't lost a game, and we had lost only one. There was a huge _____ at the game, and the fans _____ when we ran onto the field. Both teams thought that the game would be _____ and very close, but we _____ everyone by winning easily. I _____ 12 points and was the star of the game.

Discuss these questions and topics in pairs or small groups.

1. Are you a sports **fan**? If so, what sport or sports do you like?
2. When we travel, we're sometimes **amazed** by what we see. Name something that amazed you when you first saw it.
3. **Discover** often means *to find new information about a person or thing we already know.* For example, "Joe *discovered* that his friend was rich." Tell us something you discovered about a person or thing by completing this sentence.
   I discovered that _____
   _____.

4. Books, movies, and TV programs can be **exciting** or dull. Name a book, movie, or TV program that you found exciting and one that you found dull.

5. Did you ever **join** a team, club, or other group? If so, what team, club, or group did you join?

6. Many events and places, such as parades, important games, and Niagara Falls, attract crowds. Name some other events or places that attract crowds.

7. In the United States, some sports have cheerleaders, young women or men who lead the **cheers** during a game. What sports usually have cheerleaders? What sports don't? Do other countries usually have cheerleaders?

8. In different sports, there are different names for the points a player **scores**; for example, players score *goals* in soccer. In what sport do they score *runs*? In what sport do they score *touchdowns?*

WORD FAMILIES

Complete the sentences with these words. *If necessary, add an ending to the word so it forms a correct sentence.* (adj. = adjective and adv. = adverb)

1. **to amaze** (verb)   **amazing** (adj.)   **amazement** (noun)

   A. Computers work with _____ speed.

   B. You can imagine our _____ when Ralph hit his third home run in one game.

   C. New York City's skyscrapers (tall buildings) _____ visitors.

2. **to discover** (verb)   **discovery** (noun)

   A. The _____ of oil helped the Mexican economy.

   B. I wasn't happy when I _____ that the dog ate my hamburger.

3. **exciting** (adj.)   **to excite** (verb)   **excitement** (noun)

   A. It's a quiet town with very little _____.

   B. The Olympic Games _____ many fans.

   C. I really enjoyed the play. It was _____.

4. **crowd** (noun)   **crowded** (adj.)

   A. The _____ was making so much noise that I couldn't hear what my friend was saying.

   B. The store is _____ because of the big sale.

5. **to cheer** (verb)   **cheerful** (adj.)
   cheerfully (adv.)   **cheerfulness** (noun)

   A. It's spring and the birds are singing _____.

   B. When the team heard the fans _____, they played harder.

   C. Ray is a _____ person. He's always happy.

   D. The nurses' _____ helps the patients.

BUILDING WORDS WITH *RE–*

The prefix *re-* is placed before some verbs to form a new verb. For example, *re + write = rewrite; re + visit = revisit.*

The prefix *re-* means *again. Rewrite* means *to write again; revisit* means *to visit again.*

Verb	New Verb	Verb	New Verb
build	rebuild	name	rename
consider	reconsider	open	reopen
discover	rediscover	play	replay
do	redo	produce	reproduce
enter	reenter	read	reread
join	rejoin	visit	revisit
marry	remarry	write	rewrite

Circle the letter next to the word that best completes the sentence.

1. The store is closed, but it'll _____ in the morning.

   a. reproduce   c. revisit
   b. redo   d. reopen

2. Angela's husband died two years ago; but she's going to _____ soon.

   a. remarry   c. rebuild
   b. reconsider   d. rediscover

3. They decided to _____ the airport in honor of President Kennedy.

    a. reenter

    b. revisit

    c. rename

    d. reconsider

4. There are many mistakes in my letter. I'm going to _____ it.

    a. replay

    b. rewrite

    c. rebuild

    d. rediscover

5. We weren't able to spend much time at the museum. We're going to _____ it tomorrow.

    a. revisit

    b. reconsider

    c. reproduce

    d. rejoin

6. The fire completely destroyed the school, but the city is going to _____ it.

    a. rejoin

    b. reenter

    c. rebuild

    d. rediscover

7. Why don't you _____ the club? Everyone wants you to come back.

    a. reproduce

    b. rejoin

    c. rename

    d. redo

8. If you don't understand the story, you should _____ it.

    a. rediscover

    b. reopen

    c. reenter

    d. reread

USING THE INTERNET TO FIND INFORMATION

1. *Enter* the keyword **U.S. soccer** *in the search box of any general search engine such as Google or Yahoo. Click on the "search" button or hit "enter" on the keyboard. The search engine will lead you to a list of Web sites.*

   Click on the links to two or three of these Web sites. Look over these sites and choose the one that seems the most interesting and that tells you the most about U.S. soccer. Read a page or two. (Option: write down two or three things you learned about U.S. soccer from this site.)

2. *Enter* the keywords **barbers, U.S. Department of Labor** *in the search box of any general search engine such as Google or Yahoo. Click on the "search" button or hit "enter" on the keyboard. The search engine will lead you to a list of Web sites.*

   Click on the links to two or three of these Web sites. Look over these sites and choose the one that seems the most interesting and that tells you the most about barbers. Read a page or two. (Option: write down two or three things you learned about barbers from this site.)

CHAPTER 14

A Motorcycle

PREVIEW QUESTIONS

Discuss or think about these questions before reading the story.

1. Do you think it would be fun to ride a motorcycle? Explain your answer.

2. What are some of the causes of motorcycle accidents?

3. Why are motorcycle accidents worse than car accidents?

A Motorcycle

Last year Mario decided he was going to buy a motorcycle, take lessons, and get his license. Riding a motorcycle was something he always wanted to do. Two of his best friends rode motorcycles, and he wanted to ride with them. It would be exciting.

When he told Connie about the motorcycle, she was upset. She thought it was a crazy thing to do. Of course she was afraid he would have an accident. She **attempted** to change his mind. She reminded him that he had two young children. Mario replied, "I'll be a **cautious** driver; nothing will happen. My best friends drive motorcycles and they've never had an accident. You think too much."

Mario was proud of his new motorcycle, but it wasn't cheap. It cost $9,000. He took $4,000 from his savings account and borrowed the rest. He couldn't wait to ride his motorcycle and show it to his friends.

For a year, Mario rode his motorcycle without a problem. He often rode with his friends, but sometimes he rode by himself. One Sunday afternoon, he decided to go for a ride. There were some clouds in the sky, and the weather report said there was a chance of showers. But Mario didn't expect rain. He was riding his motorcycle on the highway and **suddenly** it started to rain.

The highway was slippery and Mario slowed down a little. He was only five miles from home, so he didn't stop at a diner he passed. That was a mistake. He was riding down a big hill and lost control of the motorcycle. It went off the highway and **crashed** into a large tree. Two cars stopped to help Mario. One of the drivers called 911 on his cell phone. The police and the paramedics arrived quickly. They took him to the hospital.

The motorcycle was badly **damaged**, but fortunately, Mario's injuries were **slight.** He had a few cuts and a broken nose. He was wearing a helmet at the time and that saved his life.

The accident wasn't Mario's **fault.** He wasn't speeding. The weather and the slippery highway were to **blame**, but Mario also **blamed** himself for not stopping at the diner and waiting for the rain to stop.

Connie was happy that his injuries were slight, but she asked him to stop riding his motorcycle. "You might not be so lucky the next time," she said. Mario told her he would think about stopping and let her know. What do you think he should do? What do you think he will do?

TRUE OR FALSE

If the sentence is true, write *T*. If it's false, write *F*.

_____ 1. Mario always wanted to ride a motorcycle.

_____ 2. Connie thought it was OK for Mario to buy a motorcycle.

_____ 3. Mario's motorcycle was expensive.

_____ 4. Mario thought it was going to rain.

_____ 5. He stopped at a diner.

_____ 6. It was fortunate that Mario was wearing a helmet.

_____ 7. He was driving too fast.

_____ 8. Connie wanted Mario to stop riding his motorcycle.

WHAT DO YOU THINK?

Use your experience, ideas, and the story to answer these questions.

1. Do you think it was crazy for Mario to get a motorcycle? Explain your answer.

2. Would you be afraid if someone in your family decided to get a motorcycle? Explain your answer.

3. Do you think Mario should stop riding his motorcycle or should he keep riding? Explain your answer.

4. Many people take a cell phone with them when they drive. Why is this a good idea?

GUESSING FROM CONTEXT

Guess the meaning of the key words in these sentences. *Use the context of the story to help you. Circle your answers.*

1. Connie **attempted** to change his mind.

   a. wanted   c. was not able
   b. knew how   d. tried

2. I'll be a **cautious** driver.

   a. very good   c. very careful
   b. very smart   d. very fast

3. Fortunately, Mario's injuries were **slight**.

   a. small   c. painless
   b. average   d. deep

MINI-DICTIONARY—PART ONE

WORD ENTRIES

---

at·tempt / ə-tempt′ / *verb:* to try to do something; to make an effort: *Sonia* **attempted** *to sell her car for $1,000.* —*noun:* an effort: *I couldn't do my math homework, but at least I made an* **attempt**.

cau·tious / kô′shəs / *adjective:* very careful: *Alicia is* **cautious**. *She always thinks before she acts.*

sud·den·ly / sud′ən-lē / *adverb:* happening quickly and unexpectedly: *The truck in front of us stopped* **suddenly**, *and we almost hit it.*

crash / krash / *verb:* to hit with great force, especially in an accident: *The bus* **crashed** *into a telephone poll.* —*noun:* a violent accident in a car, plane, or train: *Three people were killed in the train* **crash**.

COMPLETING SENTENCES

Complete the sentences with these words. *Use each word twice. Where a word has different endings, both forms are given.*

attempt/attempting	cautious	crash/crashed	suddenly

1. They're _____ to complete the highway by November 1, but I don't think they can.

2. Larry _____ felt sick and had to leave the room.

3. My friend was in a helicopter _____, but he didn't get hurt.

4. Pablo is slow to change. He's _____.

5. I slipped and fell on the icy sidewalk _____.

6. I thanked Emily for her _____ to get me a job.

7. My doctor is _____. He wants me to rest a few days before I go back to work.

8. The baseball player _____ into the fence trying to catch the ball.

WORD ENTRIES

dam·age / dam'ij / *verb:* to make something less valuable; to harm: *Loud music can **damage** your hearing.* —*noun:* loss of value; harm: *Hurricanes do a lot of **damage** in the Caribbean and Florida.*

slight / slīt / *adjective:* small; not serious: *Kathleen has a **slight** cold. She'll be fine in a day or two.*

fault / fôlt / *noun* **1:** responsibility for something bad: *It's my own **fault** that I did poorly on the exam. I didn't study.* **2:** a weak point in a person: *I talk too much. It's one of my **faults**.*

blame / blām / *verb:* to say someone is responsible for something bad: *The economy is doing poorly and many people **blame** the president.* —*noun:* responsibility for something bad: *Matthew is to **blame*** for the accident. He went through a red light.*
*****Blame** is frequently used in the expression *be to blame.*

COMPLETING SENTENCES

Complete the sentences with these words. *Use each word twice. Where a word has different endings, both forms are given.*

fault/faults	damage/damaged	blame/blaming	slight

1. The cold weather _____ the orange trees.

2. Jane is wonderful, but she has her _____. She isn't perfect.

3. Masako speaks English well, but she has a _____ accent.

4. The food at the restaurant was terrible. I think the cook is to _____.

5. We have to make some _____ changes in our plan.

6. How much _____ did the fire do to your house?

7. Ralph was late for work, but it wasn't his _____. His car wouldn't start.

8. Why are they _____ me? I didn't do anything wrong.

STORY COMPLETION

Discuss or think about these questions before completing the story that follows.

1. Why is there a lot of traffic at five o'clock in the afternoon?

2. Why do we have to drive carefully when passing trucks and buses?

3. Do you drive? Are you a cautious driver?

Complete the story with these words.

damaged	crashed	slight	cautious
attempted	blame	suddenly	fault

Hitting a Bus in the Rain

It was five o'clock in the afternoon when the Greyhound bus left the station in San Francisco. The bus was going down a busy street when a car _____ to pass. That was foolish. The driver _____ lost control of his car and _____ into the side of the bus.

The accident wasn't the bus driver's _____. The driver of the car was to _____. He should have been more _____, but he was in a hurry and didn't want to stay behind the bus.

Fortunately, all the people on the bus were OK. So the driver got back in the bus and continued on her way to Los Angeles.

However, the car was badly _____, and the driver had a broken arm and a _____ cut on his face. An ambulance took him to the hospital.

SHARING INFORMATION

Discuss these questions and topics in pairs or small groups.

1. Complete one of the following sentences. I **attempted** to _____, but couldn't. I **attempted** to _____ and did.

2. Which statement best describes you? A. I'm very **cautious**. B. I'm cautious. C. I'm a bit cautious. D. I'm not at all cautious.

3. Tell us about something you did **suddenly**, or that suddenly happened to you.

4. When you get on a plane, how afraid are you of a **crash?** A little? A lot? Not at all? Which do you think is safer—flying or driving in a car? Explain your answer.

5. Describe the **damage** caused by a fire, storm, or accident you were in, read about, or saw on television.

6. Some problems are big; some are **slight.** Complete one of the following sentences. I have a slight problem— _____. My friend has a slight problem— _____.

7. No one is perfect. We all have **faults.** Think of a fault that you have or that a friend has, and tell us what it is. For example, "My friend is lazy."

8. When a student does poorly in school, who is usually to **blame?** The teacher(s)? The student? The parents? No one? Explain your answer.

WORD FAMILIES

Complete the sentences with these words. *If necessary, add an ending to the word so it forms a correct sentence.* (adj. = adjective and adv. = adverb)

1. **cautious** (adj.)   **caution** (noun)   **cautiously** (adv.)

   A. They removed the bomb from the building with great _____.

   B. Dan spends his money _____.

   C. It's not enough for firefighters to be brave. They also have to be

   _____.

2. **suddenly** (adv.)   **sudden** (adj.)

   A. A _____ storm hit the coast of California.

   B. _____ the lights in our house went out.

3. **to blame** (verb)   **blameless** (adj.)

   A. The police made a mistake when they arrested Tony. He was

   _____.

   B. Our team hasn't won a game, and I _____ the coach.

4. **slight** (adj.)   **slightly** (adv.)

   A. General Motors is offering its workers a _____ pay increase.

   B. It's _____ warmer today.

BUILDING ADJECTIVES WITH -OUS

The suffix **-ous** is added to nouns and verbs to form an adjective. For example, *fame + ous = famous; space + ous = spacious; religion + ous = religious.*

The suffix **-ous** usually means *having, having a lot of,* or *having to do with. Famous* means *having fame; spacious* means *having a lot of space; religious* means *having to do with religion.*

Noun or Verb	Adjective	Noun or Verb	Adjective
advantage	advantageous	nerve	nervous
caution	cautious	number	numerous
continue	continuous	poison	poisonous
fame	famous	religion	religious
joy	joyous	space	spacious
mountain	mountainous	study	studious
mystery	mysterious		

Circle the letter next to the word that best completes the sentence.

1. I love weddings. They're _____ occasions.

   a. continuous   c. famous

   b. nervous   d. joyous

2. I know Miami well. I have made _____ trips there.

   a. mysterious   c. advantageous

   b. numerous   d. cautious

3. Jason is always in the library with his nose in a book. He's _____.

   a. studious   c. religious

   b. famous   d. nervous

4. Much of Bolivia is _____.

   a. joyous   c. mountainous

   b. cautious   d. continuous

5. That's _____. My glasses were here a minute ago, and now I don't see them.

   a. advantageous   c. mysterious

   b. continuous   d. numerous

6. Almost everyone has heard of Babe Ruth. He was a _____ baseball player.

   a. cautious   c. nervous

   b. religious   d. famous

7. You can put a lot in this room. It's _____.

   a. spacious   c. mysterious

   b. mountainous   d. continuous

8. Chris gets _____ when he has to go to a doctor.

   a. joyous   c. religious

   b. nervous   d. studious

USING THE INTERNET TO FIND INFORMATION

1. *Enter the keywords **Honda motorcycles** in the search box of any general search engine such as Google or Yahoo. Click on the "search" button or hit "enter" on the keyboard. The search engine will lead you to a list of Web sites.*

   Click on the links to two or three of these Web sites. Look over these sites and choose the one that seems the most interesting and that tells you the most about Honda motorcycles. Read a page or two. (Option: write down two or three things you learned about Honda motorcycles from this site.)

2. *Enter the keywords **motorcycle helmets save lives** in the search box of any general search engine such as Google or Yahoo. Click on the "search" button or hit "enter" on the keyboard. The search engine will lead you to a list of Web sites.*

   Click on the links to two or three of these Web sites. Look over these sites and choose the one that seems the most interesting and that tells you the most about motorcycle helmets saving lives. Read a page or two. (Option: write down two or three things you learned about motorcycle helmets from this site.)

CHAPTER 15

Cholesterol

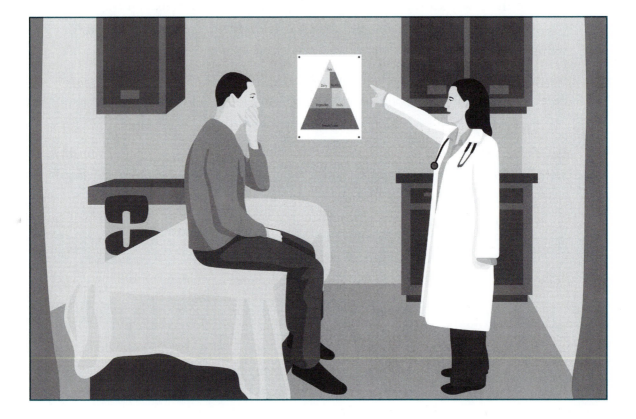

PREVIEW QUESTIONS

Discuss or think about these questions before reading the story.

1. What do you know about cholesterol?
2. Have you ever had your cholesterol checked? If so, do you remember what it was?
3. What can high cholesterol do that causes heart problems?

Cholesterol

One morning Mario felt some **pain** in his chest and arms, but the pain went away and Mario didn't **worry** about it anymore. He didn't mention the pain to Connie because he knew she would worry too much.

However, when Mario went to the doctor for his yearly checkup, the doctor discovered that Mario's total cholesterol was 260. That's high. The doctor **warned** him that high cholesterol was **dangerous** and could lead to a heart attack. He had to lower his cholesterol by changing his diet and getting more exercise. The doctor's **warning** was clear.

The doctor also explained to Mario that there are two kinds of cholesterol—HDL (high-density lipoproteins) and LDL (low-density lipoproteins). HDL is "good" cholesterol. The higher it is, the better. LDL is "bad" cholesterol. The lower it is, the better.

When Mario got home from the doctor, he said to Connie, "My cholesterol is 260, but there is nothing to worry about. I'm going to lower it by changing my diet and exercise." "You have to," she replied. "260 is too high."

Since Mario was playing on a soccer team, he was already getting a lot of exercise. The **main** thing he had to do was change his diet. But that was not going to be easy. He loved hamburgers, butter, ice cream, and cake.

The doctor gave him a three-page diet and told Mario to start the diet **right away.** Hamburgers, butter, ice cream, and cake were not on the diet. He had to eat more fruit and vegetables **instead.** They don't have any cholesterol. He also changed from regular to skim milk.

The doctor told Mario to come back in six weeks, and he would check his cholesterol again. If it didn't change, the doctor would give him medicine to lower his cholesterol. But first Mario had to try to lower his cholesterol with a diet and more exercise.

Mario wasn't happy with his new diet. Hamburgers were his favorite food and ice cream was his favorite dessert. He **used to** eat a big dish of ice cream every day. Now he eats no-fat ice cream and veggieburgers,[1] but they don't taste the same.

Continued on page 160

Continued from page 159

Mario likes fruit, especially bananas, oranges, and apples, so eating more fruit is not a problem. However, the only vegetable he likes is carrots. Connie prepares special vegetables dishes for Mario. They don't taste great, but he eats them. When he sees the doctor in six weeks, he doesn't want to hear that he has to take medicine to lower his cholesterol.

---

[1] A **veggieburger** is a burger made of vegetables instead of meat.

COMPREHENSION QUESTIONS

Answer these questions about the story. *Use your experience and own ideas to answer questions with an asterisk (*). Work in pairs or small groups. The numbers in parentheses tell you which paragraph in the story has the answer.*

1. Why didn't Mario mention his pain to Connie? (1)

2. What did the doctor say about high cholesterol? (2)

3. Name the two kinds of cholesterol that the doctor explained. (3)

*4. Do you think that Mario was worried about his high cholesterol? Explain your answer.

5. What was the main thing that Mario had to do? (5)

6. When did the doctor want Mario to start his diet? (6)

7. What did Mario have to eat in place of hamburgers, butter, ice cream, and cake? (6)

*8. Why is skim milk better than regular milk for people with high cholesterol?

9. If Mario's cholesterol doesn't come down, what is the doctor going to do? (7)

10. What was Mario's favorite food? What was his favorite dessert? (8)

11. What fruits does Mario especially like? What vegetable does he like? (9)

*12. Why do you think Mario doesn't want to take medicine to lower his cholesterol?

Guess the meaning of the key words in these sentences. *Use the context of the story to help you. Circle your answers.*

1. The doctor warned Mario that high cholesterol was **dangerous**.

   a. foolish   c. necessary

   b. poison   d. not safe

2. The **main** thing Mario had to do was change his diet.

   a. most difficult   c. most important

   b. only   d. most exciting

3. The doctor told Mario to start the diet **right away**.

   a. tomorrow   c. soon

   b. immediately   d. when he wanted to

MINI-DICTIONARY—PART ONE

WORD ENTRIES

> **main** / mān / *adjective:* the most important and often the largest: *In the United States, most people eat their **main** meal in the evening.*
>
> **warn** / wôrn / *verb:* to say that something is dangerous or may be a problem: *I **warned** the children not to play in the street.*
>
> **warn·ing** / wôr'ning / *noun:* a statement that something is dangerous or may be a problem: *The police officer gave me a **warning** not to drive so fast.*
>
> **used to** / yōōs tōō *or* yōōs'tə / *idiom:* done in the past, but not done now; true in the past, but not true now: *Mi Sook **used to** live in Korea. Now she lives in San Francisco.*
>
> **dan·ger·ous** / dān'jər-əs / *adjective:* likely to hurt someone; not safe: *The road is **dangerous**. It's narrow and has many curves.*

COMPLETING SENTENCES

Complete the sentences with these words. *Use each word twice. Where a word has different endings, both forms are given.*

dangerous	main	warned/warning	used to

1. Where is the _____ entrance to the school?

2. Texas _____ be part of Mexico.

3. Walking in the park late at night is _____.

4. In 1941, Japan attacked the United States without _____.

5. The city has three libraries. The _____ one is in the center of the city.

6. The teacher _____ us that the test would be hard.

7. Ellen is a firefighter. Her job is _____.

8. I _____ play the piano, but I don't anymore.

MINI-DICTIONARY—PART TWO

WORD ENTRIES

pain / pān / *noun:* a very uncomfortable feeling; suffering: *The **pain** in my arm is bad. I'm going to see a doctor.*

wor·ry / wûr'ē / *verb:* to be afraid that something bad happened or may happen: *My husband is a police officer, and I **worry** about him.* —*noun:* a fear that something bad happened or may happen: *When I play tennis, I forget my **worries**.*

right a·way / rīt ə-wā' / *adverb:* immediately; now: *The ambulance came **right away**. We didn't have to wait long.*

in·stead / in-sted' / *adverb:* in place of that: *We wanted to go swimming, but it was too cold. So we went for a walk **instead**.*

instead of / in-sted'əv / *preposition:* in place of: *I'm going to drink tea **instead of** coffee.*

COMPLETING SENTENCES

Complete the sentences with these words. *Use each word twice. Where a word has different endings, both forms are given.*

worry/worries	right away	pain	instead/instead of

1. Paula is very busy, but she answered my e-mail _____.
2. Carl and Lauren were going to watch TV, but they played cards _____.
3. Hector plays football, and his mother _____ that he might get hurt.
4. Take two aspirin, and the _____ will go away.
5. I'm going to have potatoes _____ rice.
6. The show is going to start _____.
7. Walter has a _____ in his back. He's going to stay home and rest.
8. I don't have a job and I can't find one. It's a big _____.

STORY COMPLETION

Discuss or think about these questions before completing the story that follows.

1. Do you like boxing? Have you ever watched it on TV? Have you ever gone to a boxing match?
2. Professional boxing is dangerous; for example, some boxers suffer brain damage. How can boxing be made safer?
3. Do you think the government should stop all boxing? Pass laws to make it safer? Do nothing? Explain your answer.

Complete the story with these words.

main	instead	warned	pain
used to	worry	right away	dangerous

A Young Boxer

Bill Green _____ be a boxer, and he was one of the best young boxers in the state of New York. However, his parents didn't want him to box, and they _____ him to quit before he got hurt. He knew that boxing was _____, but he told his parents not to _____. He was strong and healthy and a very good boxer.

163

One night, Bill was fighting a bigger and faster boxer. It was an important fight for both boxers and the _____ fight of the evening. Late in the fight, Bill got a cut over his left eye. It was deep and the _____ was very bad. He could hardly see out of his left eye. The referee stopped the fight _____.

Bill had planned to go to a victory party after he won the fight, but they had to take him to the hospital _____. Bill's eye is going to be OK, but he's not going to box anymore. His parents are very happy about that.

SHARING INFORMATION

Discuss these questions and topics in pairs or small groups.

1. Some sports are **dangerous.** Others are safe. Name three dangerous sports and three safe ones.

2. What is your **main** reason for studying English? What are some other reasons?

3. Every pack of cigarettes and all cigarette ads **warn** people that smoking is dangerous. Do you think these **warnings** help? Do they keep some people from smoking? Do they make others think about quitting?

4. Complete the following sentence. I **used to** live in _____; now I live in _____.

5. When we think of **pain,** we usually think of physical pain. But pain can also be emotional or psychological. Name some things that cause emotional or psychological pain, such as losing a job.

6. Everyone **worries.** Name three things people worry about.

7. When you wake up in the morning and it's time to get up, do you usually get up **right away,** or do you usually stay in bed a while?

8. Complete the following sentences. _____ is my favorite drink. But if I want a change, I drink _____ **instead.**

WORD FAMILIES

Complete the sentences with these words. *If necessary, add an ending to the word so it forms a correct sentence.* (adj. = adjective and adv. = adverb)

1. **dangerous** (adj.)   **danger** (noun)   **dangerously** (adv.)

   A. If you put your money in the bank, there is no _____ of losing it.

   B. That car came _____ close to us.

   C. Arguing with your boss can be _____.

2. **main** (adj.)   **mainly** (adv.)

   A. I like all kinds of music, but I'm _____ interested in rock.

   B. Ms. Trawinsky is going to be the _____ speaker at the conference.

3. **pain** (noun)   **painful** (adj.)   **painless** (adj.)

   A. I was lucky. The tests I had in the hospital were _____.

   B. I have a toothache, and the _____ is killing me.

   C. Janet's sunburn is very _____.

4. **instead** (adv.)   **instead of** (preposition)

   A. I was going to visit my cousin, but I phoned her _____.

   B. Lester is on a diet, so he ate an apple _____ a piece of cake.

BUILDING NOUNS WITH -ING

The suffix **-ing** is added to many verbs to form a noun. For example, *run + ing = running; read + ing = reading; paint + ing = painting.*

The suffix **-ing** means *the action of.* For example, *running* means *the action of running; reading* means *the action of reading; painting* means *the action of painting.*

Verb	Noun	Verb	Noun
begin	beginning	read	reading
farm	farming	run	running
feel	feeling	suffer	suffering
hear	hearing	swim	swimming
hunt	hunting	understand	understanding
meet	meeting	warn	warning
paint	painting	write	writing

Circle the letter next to the word that best completes the sentence.

1. Pete is moving from the country to the city. He doesn't like _____.

   a. swimming   c. farming
   b. running   d. reading

2. You'll have to speak louder. My _____ is poor.

   a. beginning   c. reading
   b. hearing   d. painting

3. Monica has a clear _____ of the problem and a plan to solve it.

   a. understanding   c. feeling
   b. writing   d. warning

4. The _____ of the play is very funny.

   a. meeting   c. painting
   b. hunting   d. beginning

5. I have a _____ that it's going to snow.

   a. hearing   c. understanding
   b. feeling   d. reading

6. _____ is the most important skill children learn when they start school.

   a. Reading   c. Farming
   b. Swimming   d. Painting

7. _____ is good exercise and fun.

   a. Meeting   c. Writing
   b. Understanding   d. Swimming

8. The teachers talked for three hours about ways to improve the school. It was a long _____.

   a. warning   c. meeting
   b. suffering   d. beginning

1. *Enter* the keyword **cholesterol** *in the search box of any general search engine such as Google or Yahoo. Click on the "search" button or hit "enter" on the keyboard. The search engine will lead you to a list of Web sites.*

   Click on the links to two or three of these Web sites. Look over these sites and choose the one that seems the most interesting and that tells you the most about cholesterol. Read a page or two. (Option: write down two or three things you learned about cholesterol from this site.)

2. *Enter* the keywords **diet and cholesterol** *in the search box of any general search engine such as Google or Yahoo. Click on the "search" button or hit "enter" on the keyboard. The search engine will lead you to a list of Web sites.*

   Click on the links to two or three of these Web sites. Look over these sites and choose the one that seems the most interesting and that tells you the most about diet and cholesterol. Read a page or two. (Option: write down two or three things you learned about diet and cholesterol from this site.)

SYNONYMS

Next to each sentence, write the word that has the same meaning or almost the same meaning as the part of the sentence in bold print.

cheered	slight	attempting	main
crowd	suddenly	amazed	cautious

1. _____ When I drive in snow, I'm **very careful**.
2. _____ The baby is **trying** to walk, but her legs aren't strong enough yet.
3. _____ A **large number of people** came to watch the parade.
4. _____ What is the **most important** idea of this paragraph?
5. _____ Toyota announced a **small** increase in the price of their cars.
6. _____ We were **very surprised** that Brett spoke French, Italian, and Spanish.
7. _____ Everyone **shouted** when our team scored a touchdown.
8. _____ The door opened **quickly and unexpectedly**.

SENTENCE COMPLETION

Complete the sentences with these words.

fault	score	worry	damage
fans	blame	exciting	warned

1. My son is doing poorly in school, and I think his teacher is to _____.
2. Shirley _____ me not to trust Jerry. I'm sorry I didn't listen to her.
3. We lost the game, but the _____ was close.
4. The children had a very _____ day at the zoo.

5. I have a headache, and it's my own _____. I drank too much wine at the party.

6. Len enjoys life, and he doesn't _____ about anything.

7. Many _____ stayed home from the game because of the rain.

8. At the end of the school year, the students have to return their books and pay for any _____.

STORY COMPLETION

Complete the story with these words.

crashed	discovered	pain	dangerous
instead	used to	joining	right away

Skiing

Skiing is a _____ sport, and no one knows this better than Ivan. He _____ ski a lot, but last winter he had a bad accident.

He was skiing down the side of a mountain, and he _____ into a tree. Ivan was in a lot of _____, so they took him to a hospital _____. They _____ that he had broken both of his legs.

This winter Ivan isn't going to do any skiing. He plans to swim _____. So he's _____ a swim club.

New Jobs for Women

CHAPTER 16

A Police Officer

PREVIEW QUESTIONS

Discuss or think about these questions before reading the story.

1. Why is it important that police departments have women officers?

2. What do you think police officers have to learn before they start their job?

3. How do you think most parents feel about having a son or daughter join the police department?

A Police Officer

When Nancy finished high school, she didn't want to go to college. Her parents said that was OK, but they didn't want her sitting around the house doing nothing. **Therefore,** she had to work or go to school. Since Nancy wanted to work and make some money, that was fine with her. She got a job at a bank and worked as a teller for four years. The job was interesting for a while because everything was new and she learned a lot.

Nancy, however, had always wanted to be a police officer. But she was only 17 when she graduated from high school, and that was too young. So she waited until she was 21. Then she made an **appointment** to talk to an officer at the police department.

Nancy was a little nervous when she talked to the officer, but he was kind and that helped her relax. He said the department didn't have enough female police officers, and that she should **apply.** He warned her that the job was difficult and that she would have to take both written and physical exams. She applied and did very well on the exams.

Six weeks later, Nancy received an appointment to the police department. She was so excited she could hardly wait to tell her friends. Everyone at the bank wished her well and said they would miss her. Naturally, she was **eager** to begin, but first she had to go to the police academy for six months to learn about state and local laws, about the best way to handle people, and about how and when to use a gun. The academy was **rather** difficult, but Nancy completed her courses without too much trouble.

Nancy's parents didn't like the idea of her becoming a police officer. They said that the job was too dangerous. They **suggested** that she become a computer programmer. She liked to work with computers and knew a lot about them. Her parents said they would pay to send Nancy to school to learn more about computers, and then she could get a safe job.

Nancy **replied**, "I'm **aware** of the dangers, but I want to be a police officer, not a computer programmer. My job will be exciting and important. It'll give me a chance to help people and to make our streets safer. Besides, I'm 21; it's my decision." But to her parents, she was still very young, and they were afraid.

Answer these questions about the story. *Use your experience and own ideas to answer questions with an asterisk (*). Work in pairs or small groups. The numbers in parentheses tell you which paragraph in the story has the answer.*

1. What did Nancy's parents say about her not going to college? (1)

*2. Do you think they were unhappy about her not going to college? Explain your answer.

3. Why didn't Nancy become a police officer when she graduated from high school? (2)

4. Who did she make an appointment with? (2)

5. How did she feel when she talked to the officer? (3)

6. What warning did he give her? (3)

7. How did she feel when she learned about her appointment to the police department? (4)

8. Name three things they taught her in the police academy? (4)

9. What did Nancy's parents want her to become? (5)

*10. Do you think Nancy will have an opportunity to use her knowledge of computers in the police department? Explain your answer.

11. Why does she want to be a police officer? (6)

*12. Do you think she understands her parents' fears, or do you think she's angry at them? Explain your answer.

GUESSING FROM CONTEXT

Guess the meaning of the key words in these sentences. *Use the context of the story to help you. Circle your answers.*

1. Her parents didn't want her sitting around the house doing nothing. **Therefore**, she had to work or go to school.

   a. soon
   b. that's why
   c. but
   d. fortunately

2. Naturally, she **was eager** to begin, but first she had to go to the police academy.

   a. was foolish
   b. was slow
   c. was proud
   d. wanted very much

3. Nancy replied, "**I'm aware of** the dangers, but I want to be a police officer, not a computer programmer."

    a. I know of

    b. I'm unhappy about

    c. I'm afraid of

    d. I'm hesitant because of

MINI-DICTIONARY—PART ONE

WORD ENTRIES

there·fore / thâr′fôr / *adverb:* for that reason; that is why; so: *Tomorrow is a holiday.* **Therefore,** *I don't have to go to work.*

ap·point·ment / ə-point′mənt / *noun* **1:** an agreement to meet with someone at a definite time and place: *What time is your* **appointment** *with the doctor?* **2:** the placing of a person in a job: *Rita just received an* **appointment** *to teach history at Boston College.*

ap·ply / ə-plī′ / *verb:* to ask for something formally, especially by filling out a form: *I'm* **applying** *for a Sears credit card.*

ea·ger / ē′gər / *adjective:* having a strong desire to: *Peggy is a good student. She's* **eager** *to learn.*

COMPLETING SENTENCES

Complete the sentences with these words. *Use each word twice. Where a word has different endings, both forms are given.*

appointment	applying/applied	therefore	eager

1. Jeff has been in the hospital for ten days. He's _____ to go home.

2. Kim _____ for a visa to visit the United States, but she hasn't received it yet.

3. Mrs. Robinson is very busy. You have to have an _____ to see her.

4. Darryl is rich. _____, he can buy almost anything he wants.

5. Kevin was happy about his _____ to be the coach of the high-school football team.

6. The boss likes Stan because he's an _____ worker.

7. I'm on a diet. _____ , I'm not having dessert.

8. Jackie wants to go to college, but her family doesn't have much money. She's _____ for financial aid.

MINI-DICTIONARY—PART TWO

WORD ENTRIES

> **rath·er** / rath'ər / *adverb:* somewhat; quite: *It's raining **rather** hard.* (Note: *very* is stronger than *rather.*)
>
> **sug·gest** / sə-jest' *or* seg-jest' / *verb:* to say that it is a good idea to do or consider something: *Andy fell on the sidewalk and broke his leg. I **suggested** that he see a lawyer.*
>
> **re·ply** / ri-plī' / *verb:* to answer: *I don't think the president will **reply** to that question.* —*noun:* an answer: *We invited Amy and Scott to our wedding, and we're waiting for a **reply.***
>
> **a·ware** / ə-wâr' / *adjective:* having knowledge of something: *Are you **aware** that John and Mohammad are good friends?*

COMPLETING SENTENCES

Complete the sentences with these words. *Use each word twice. Where a word has different endings, both forms are given.*

rather	aware	reply/replied	suggest/suggested

1. The doctor _____ that I lose 20 pounds and get more exercise.

2. I wasn't _____ that Aaron liked to cook.

3. We asked the mayor to speak at our high school graduation, and he _____ that he was busy that night.

4. It's a big house, but the kitchen is _____ small.

5. Was Judy _____ that her son was using drugs?

6. Can you _____ the name of a good restaurant near here? We don't know where to eat.

7. This magazine is _____ interesting. I like it.

8. I wrote to my sister two weeks ago, but I haven't received a _____ yet.

Discuss or think about these questions before completing the story that follows.

1. Do you like math?
2. Do (did) you do well in math in school?
3. Did a teacher ever call your parents? If so, why?

Complete the story with these words.

applied	therefore	eager	rather
suggested	replies	appointment	aware

Math and Marks

Eric is in his last year in high school, and he hopes to graduate in June. However, he did poorly on his first math test and worse on his second. And both tests were _____ easy. _____, the math teacher phoned his parents and made a (an) _____ to see them. Eric wasn't happy about the phone call or the meeting, but he knew it was his own fault that he was failing math.

Eric's parents and math teacher discussed the problem for an hour. The teacher said that Eric wasn't paying attention in class and wasn't doing his homework. She _____ that he spend an hour every night doing his homework and studying math. When Eric's parents got home, they told him he had to pay attention in class and do his homework. So he is spending a lot more time on math, and his work is improving.

Eric is _____ to go to college, but his marks are low. He's _____ that it won't be easy to get into a good college. He _____ to four colleges and hopes that one will take him. He's waiting for their _____.

SHARING INFORMATION

Discuss these questions and topics in pairs or small groups.

1. Complete this sentence. I want to learn more English; **therefore**, I _____
   _____.

2. People make **appointments** to see doctors. Who else do people make appointments with?

3. When you **apply** for a job, you have to fill out an application. What questions are usually on a job application?

4. Complete this sentence. I'm **eager** to _____
   _____.

5. **Rather** means *to some degree;* **very** means *to a high degree.* Complete these sentences with *rather* or *very.*

   1. It's _____ cold in Alaska in the winter.
   2. Bert is six feet tall. He's _____ tall.
   3. This dress costs 500 dollars. It's _____ expensive.
   4. I have to walk a mile to school. That's _____ far.

6. Anne has to buy a car and has $5,000 in the bank. She can buy a used car for $5,000, or get a loan and buy a new one costing much more. Which would you **suggest?** Explain your answer.

7. When you get an invitation, letter, or other mail that requires a **reply**, do you usually reply quickly, or do you wait until you have to reply?

8. Complete this question. Are you **aware** that I _____?

WORD FAMILIES

Complete the sentences with these words. *If necessary, add an ending to the word so it forms a correct sentence.* (adj. = adjective and adv. = adverb)

1. **appointment** (noun)　　**to appoint** (verb)

    A. The company is going to _____ a new president soon.

    B. Josh and his wife have an _____ to see a marriage counselor.

2. **to apply** (verb)　　**application** (noun)　　**applicant** (noun)

    A. I filled out a job _____ and gave it to the secretary.

    B. The college has so many _____ that it can accept only 30 percent of them.

    C. Ron is _____ to become a member of our club.

3. **eager** (adj.)　　**eagerly** (adv.)　　**eagerness** (noun)

    A. It has been a long winter, and we're _____ waiting for spring.

    B. I was in the hospital for a week, and I noticed the _____ of the nurses to help the patients.

    C. Diana and Elliot are _____ to move into their new house.

4. **to suggest** (verb)　　**suggestion** (noun)

    A. I was talking to the music teacher after class, and she _____ that I take piano lessons.

    B. We don't know where to go on our vacation. Do you have any _____?

5. **aware** (adj.)　　**awareness** (noun)

    A. The discussion increased the students' _____ of the advantages of a college education.

    B. I hope you're _____ of the dangers of drinking and driving.

BUILDING WORDS WITH IN-

The prefix **in-** is placed before some adjectives and nouns to form a new word. For example, *in + correct = incorrect; in + dependent = independent*.

The prefix **in-** means *not*. *Incorrect* means *not correct; independent* means *not dependent*.

Adjective or Noun	New Word	Adjective or Noun	New Word
active	inactive	experience	inexperience
complete	incomplete	formal	informal
correct	incorrect	frequent	infrequent
definite	indefinite	human	inhuman
dependent	independent	secure	insecure
direct	indirect	sufficient	insufficient
expensive	inexpensive	visible	invisible

Circle the letter next to the word that best completes the sentence.

1. Mary Beth does whatever she wants. She's an _____ person.

   a. inactive
   b. independent
   c. insecure
   d. invisible

2. Arnold didn't finish his report. It's _____.

   a. incorrect
   b. informal
   c. indefinite
   d. incomplete

3. The governor doesn't believe in the death penalty. He thinks it's
   _____.

   a. inhuman
   b. insufficient
   c. infrequent
   d. inactive

4. I don't have a lot of money, so I'm going to buy an _____ watch.

   a. incorrect
   b. incomplete
   c. inexpensive
   d. invisible

5. It's an _____ restaurant. You don't need a tie or jacket.

   a. informal
   b. insufficient
   c. independent
   d. indefinite

6. The little girl cries when her mother leaves her. She's _____.

   a. incorrect
   b. inactive
   c. indirect
   d. insecure

7. We need more food for the picnic. What we have is _____.

    a. inhuman   c. insufficient

    b. incorrect   d. infrequent

8. The teacher said my answer was _____, but I still think it's right.

    a. insecure   c. invisible

    b. incorrect   d. inactive

USING THE INTERNET TO FIND INFORMATION

1. *Enter the keywords **bank tellers, U.S. Department of Labor** in the search box of any general search engine such as Google or Yahoo. Click on the "search" button or hit "enter" on the keyboard. The search engine will lead you to a list of Web sites.*

   Click on the links to two or three of these Web sites. Look over these sites and choose the one that seems the most interesting and that tells you the most about bank tellers. Read a page or two. (Option: write down two or three things you learned about bank tellers from this site.)

2. *Enter the keywords **police officers, U.S. Department of Labor** in the search box of any general search engine such as Google or Yahoo. Click on the "search" button or hit "enter" on the keyboard. The search engine will lead you to a list of Web sites.*

   Click on the links to two or three of these Web sites. Look over these sites and choose the one that seems the most interesting and that tells you the most about police officers. Read a page or two. (Option: write down two or three things you learned about police officers from this site.)

CHAPTER 17

Help! Help!

PREVIEW QUESTIONS

Discuss or think about these questions before reading the story.

1. Do you like to go for walks in the park?

2. Is it safe to walk in most parks during the day? At night?

3. Do you trust most people? Or only a few? Explain your answer.

Help! Help!

Mrs. Romano teaches the third grade at Number Six School. She left school at 3:30 and decided to go for a short walk in the park before going home. It was a warm spring day and Mrs. Romano was tired. After her walk, she sat on a bench to relax. She was enjoying the **mild** weather and watching the children play baseball. There wasn't a cloud in the sky.

A tall, thin man **approached** Mrs. Romano. She's very friendly and trusts everyone. She looked up at the man and smiled; she wasn't afraid. But the man had a gun and **threatened** to shoot Mrs. Romano if she didn't give him her handbag. He was a **thief.** He took the handbag, warned her not to call for help, and ran.

Mrs. Romano was smart enough to keep quiet while the thief was near her. She had only 20 dollars in her handbag, but she had a lot of credit cards, all of her keys, and some important papers in it. And she was angry.

Mrs. Romano waited about ten seconds as the thief ran away. Then she shouted, "Help! help! That man is **stealing** my handbag!" A man, who was jogging, heard her and **chased** the thief, but it was too late. The thief was fast. The jogger had a cell phone and called 911. The 911 operator sent a police car to the park.

Nancy, the new police officer, received the called from the 911 operator, but by the time she **reached** the park, the thief was gone. Nancy **recognized** Mrs. Romano immediately. She was Nancy's third grade teacher. "I didn't know you were a police officer," Mrs. Romano said. "It's so good to see you again!"

Nancy gave Mrs. Romano a big hug and asked her to describe the thief. "He was wearing a blue jacket and gray pants. He's quite tall and has long brown hair. I can still see his face. I will recognize him if I see him again," Mrs. Romano said. "Don't worry, Mrs. Romano," Nancy replied. "We'll get him and we'll get your handbag back."

Nancy and Mrs. Romano rode around the neighborhood looking for the thief. After about an hour, Mrs. Romano suddenly saw a man in a blue jacket coming out of a bar. It was the thief. Nancy found the handbag in the man's car, so she arrested him and took him to the police station. He's in jail now and Mrs. Romano is happy to have her keys and papers back. And, of course, she's proud of her third grade student.

TRUE OR FALSE

If the sentence is true, write *T*. If it's false, write *F*.

_____ 1. After school, Mrs. Romano went for a walk in the park.

_____ 2. She didn't trust the tall, thin man who approached her.

_____ 3. The thief threatened to shoot Mrs. Romano if she didn't give him her handbag.

_____ 4. She had a lot of money in her handbag.

_____ 5. A police officer heard Mrs. Romano's shout for help and chased the thief.

_____ 6. Nancy had a special reason for hugging Mrs. Romano.

_____ 7. Nancy said she would catch the thief and return Mrs. Romano's handbag.

_____ 8. The thief threw away Mrs. Romano's handbag.

WHAT DO YOU THINK?

Use your experience, judgment, and the story to answer these questions.

1. Do you think Mrs. Romano will trust others less in the future? Explain your answer.

2. Why was it especially important for Mrs. Romano to get her keys back?

3. What should a person do if he or she loses a credit card(s)?

4. Do you think it was foolish for the jogger to chase the thief? Explain your answer.

Guess the meaning of the key words in these sentences. *Use the context of the story to help you. Circle your answers.*

1. A tall, thin man **approached** Mrs. Romano.

   a. looked at   c. came up to
   b. offered to help   d. talked to

2. Then Mrs. Romano shouted, "Help! help! That man is **stealing** my handbag!"

   a. opening   c. searching
   b. damaging   d. taking

3. A man, who was jogging, heard her and **chased** the thief, but it was too late.

   a. stopped   c. caught
   b. ran after   d. fought with

MINI-DICTIONARY—PART ONE

WORD ENTRIES

mild / mīld / *adjective:* gentle; not strong or bitter tasting; not severe: *Florida has hot summers and **mild** winters.*

ap·proach / ə-prōch′ / *verb:* to come near a person or thing: *The plane is **approaching** the airport.* —*noun* **1:** the act of coming near a person or thing: *I can't wait for the end of winter and the **approach** of spring.* **2:** a method or way of doing something: *The doctor suggested she find a new approach to help her relax.*

thief / thēf / *noun:* a person who takes things that belong to another: *The **thief** entered the house through a window. The doors were locked.*

threat·en / thret′ən / *verb:* to tell someone you may punish or hurt him or her: *I may lose my job. The manager **threatened** to fire me.*

COMPLETING SENTENCES

Complete the sentences with these words. *Use each word twice. Where a word has different endings, both forms are given.*

approach	threatens/threatened	mild	thief

1. Dorothy has a _____ case of the flu. It's nothing to worry about.

2. I want a pay increase, but I'm afraid to _____ the boss.

3. A _____ broke into my apartment and took my stereo and TV.

4. Sometimes Robin's teacher _____ to send her to the principal. Robin talks too much and doesn't do any work.

5. I like this cheese. It's _____.

6. Was your son serious when he _____ to leave home?

7. I didn't take your money. I'm not a _____.

8. Our math teacher is trying a new _____ this year.

MINI-DICTIONARY—PART TWO

WORD ENTRIES

steal / stēl / *verb*:* to take what belongs to another without permission: *Never leave money in your desk. Someone may* **steal** *it.*
*The past tense of **steal** is **stole**.

chase / chās / *verb:* to run after someone or something: *The cat is* **chasing** *a mouse.* —*noun:* an act of chasing: *The police caught the man after a long* **chase***.*

reach / rēch / *verb* **1:** to arrive at; to come to: *It took us four hours to* **reach** *the top of the mountain.* **2:** to extend one's arm and hand to touch or get something: *Put the medicine where the children can't* **reach** *it.*

rec·og·nize / rek'əg-nīz / *verb·* to remember someone or something one has not seen for a long time: *Ken had not seen Virginia for 20 years, but he* **recognized** *her immediately.*

COMPLETING SENTENCES

Complete the sentences with these words. *Use each word twice. Where a word has different endings, both forms are given.*

reach/reached	steals/stole	chase/chased	recognize/recognized

1. Brian _____ the baseball after it went over his head.

2. It was very dark, but I _____ my friend's voice.

3. They broke into the office last night and _____ our computers.

4. Can you get the flour for me? I can't _____ that high.

5. My dog likes to _____ rabbits and squirrels.

6. I left my bicycle in the yard. I hope no one _____ it.

7. We left New York City at 10:00 in the morning and _____ Washington at 2:00 in the afternoon.

8. We have made so many changes in our apartment. You won't _____ it.

STORY COMPLETION

Discuss or think about these questions before completing the story.

1. Has anyone ever stolen anything from you?

2. What did the person steal?

3. Did you get back what was stolen?

Complete the story with these words.

reconize	chased	mild	threatens
thief	approaching	reaches	steal

A Detective

Steve is a detective in the New York Police Department. He had a _____ heart attack three weeks ago and returned to work yesterday morning. He started working on the case of Jerry Smith. Jerry is a _____. He will _____ anything, but he prefers money and expensive cars. He loves to rob banks and this is how he does it.

As Jerry is _____ the entrance to a bank, he puts on a ski mask. He doesn't want anyone to _____ him. He walks up to a teller, _____ into his pocket, and pulls out a gun. He makes the teller fill a bag with cash and _____ to shoot anyone who calls the police. He takes the bag and runs out of the bank.

Yesterday, Steve got a call from a bank. Jerry was entering a bank only a few blocks from the police station. Steve rushed to the bank and got there just as Jerry was leaving. He _____ Jerry for five blocks, caught him, and arrested him. Jerry is in jail now and will probably be there for ten years. He wishes he never got into the business of stealing.

SHARING INFORMATION

Discuss these questions and topics in pairs or small groups.

1. Onions, pepper, and garlic make food hot and spicy. Do you like spicy food, or do you like food that's **mild?**

2. Some people are easy to **approach;** others are difficult to approach. What makes a person easy to approach? What makes a person difficult to approach?

3. What do banks do to protect themselves and their tellers from **thieves** like Alex and Sam?

4. Sometimes parents **threaten** their children. For example, they say, "If you don't clean your room, you can't watch TV tonight." Give another example of a threat parents make. What happens if parents threaten a lot and then do nothing when their children don't listen?

5. People usually **steal** things, but they also steal ideas. Give an example of stealing ideas.

6. Movies and TV shows often have **chases**, especially car chases. Why do movies and TV shows have so many chases?

7. What are some things that parents should lock up or put in a place where small children can't **reach** them?

8. If you met someone who hadn't seen you for many years, for example, your first grade teacher or an old friend, do you think that person would **recognize** you? Or have you changed too much?

WORD FAMILIES

Complete the sentences with these words. *If necessary, add an ending to the word so it forms a correct sentence.* (adj. = adjective and adv. = adverb)

1. **mild** (adj.)   **mildly** (adv.)

   A. Roy had a _____ headache.
   B. I was only _____ interested in Sue's story.

2. **to approach** (verb)   **approachable** (adj.)

   A. We can talk to our teacher about anything. She's very _____.
   B. The hurricane is _____ the Dominican Republic and Haiti.

3. **to threaten** (verb)   **threat** (noun)

   A. Mrs. Morales _____ to keep her class after school.
   B. Everyone had to leave the building because of a bomb _____.

4. **to recognize** (verb)   **recognition** (noun)

   A. Gabrielle works very hard for the company. She should get more _____ and a pay increase.
   B. When I saw Dick's picture in the paper, I _____ him immediately.

BUILDING VERBS WITH -*EN*

The suffix *-en* is added to some adjectives and nouns to form a verb. For example, *fright + en = frighten; sweet + en = sweeten; threat + en = threaten.*

The suffix *-en* means *to cause, to cause to be,* or *to make. Frighten* means *to cause fright; sweeten* means *to cause to be sweet; threaten* means *to make a threat.*

Adjective or Noun	Verb	Adjective or Noun	Verb
deep	deepen	soft	soften
fright	frighten	strength	strengthen
hard	harden	sweet	sweeten
length	lengthen	threat	threaten
less	lessen	weak	weaken
sad	sadden	wide	widen
short	shorten		

Circle the letter next to the word that best completes the sentence.

1. Exercise will _____ your body.

   a. deepen   c soften
   b. strengthen   d. widen

2. The road is narrow, but there are plans to _____ it.

   a. widen   c. lessen
   b. harden   d. lengthen

3. The death of our friend _____ us.

   a. softened   c. deepened
   b. hardened   d. saddened

4. The field is dry and hard; we need some rain to _____ it.

   a. lengthen   c. soften
   b. strengthen   d. deepen

5. What do they put in diet soda to _____ it?

   a. sweeten   c. harden
   b. weaken   d. lessen

6. The loud noise _____ the dog and she ran away.

   a. weakened   c. saddened
   b. strengthened   d. frightened

7. If you put the ice cream in the freezer, it'll _____ quickly.

   a. lengthen   c harden
   b. widen   d. deepen

8. The play is too long. The director should _____ it.

   a. soften   c. weaken
   b. shorten   d. widen

USING THE INTERNET TO FIND INFORMATION

1. *Enter* the keywords **elementary and secondary schoolteachers, U.S. Department of Labor** *in the search box of any general search engine such as Google or Yahoo. Click on the "search" button or hit "enter" on the keyboard. The search engine will lead you to a list of Web sites.*

   Click on the links to two or three of these Web sites. Look over these sites and choose the one that seems the most interesting and that tells you the most about schoolteachers. Read a page or two. (Option: write down two or three things you learned about schoolteachers from this site.)

2. *Enter* the keywords **how cell phones work** *in the search box of any general search engine such as Google or Yahoo. Click on the "search" button or hit "enter" on the keyboard. The search engine will lead you to a list of Web sites.*

   Click on the links to two or three of these Web sites. Look over these sites and choose the one that seems the most interesting and that tells you the most about cell phones. Read a page or two. (Option: write down two or three things you learned about cell phones from this site.)

CHAPTER 18

A Lot of Courage

PREVIEW QUESTIONS

Discuss or think about these questions before reading the story.

1. Tell what you expect of a good police officer by completing this sentence. A good police officer should _____.

2. What are the advantages of having women police officers?

3. Do you think there are any disadvantages?

A Lot of Courage

Nancy works in a small city in Pennsylvania. It's not the kind of city that likes change. So, when the city first hired female police officers, many people **wondered** if it was a good idea. "Would women be strong enough and **tough** enough to do the job," they asked. Would male police officers accept women officers?

Today, most people in the city are happy they have women police officers. But not everyone feels that way. There are still some who prefer male officers. Nancy knows this, but it doesn't **bother** her.

At first, Nancy's **partner** didn't like the idea of working with a woman, but he doesn't feel that way now. One night Dave and Nancy were working in a dangerous part of town, and he attempted to arrest a man selling drugs. The drug dealer took Dave's gun and was going to shoot him. Nancy was 30 feet away and didn't hesitate. She shot the dealer and saved Dave's life.

When Dave returned to the police station, he said to the captain, "Nancy is one of our best police officers. She has a lot of **courage** and isn't afraid of danger. She's willing to take **risks** but doesn't take foolish ones. She saved my life."

Nancy also works well with the other police officers. She smiles and laughs easily and is always pleasant. That makes it easy for them to accept her. However, she knows how to be tough and sometimes her job requires it.

Nancy is a **successful** police officer because she knows when to be kind and when to be tough. She knows when to stop a car and give a driver a ticket and when to give a warning instead. She knows when to use her gun and when not to. She doesn't like to use force, but uses it when necessary.

Nancy loves her job and never misses work, but her mom and dad still worry about her. They don't relax until she gets home and they know she's safe. But they also see how happy she is and that she's a good police officer, and, of course, they are proud of her **success.**

Today only a few people in the city wonder if it's good to have women police officers. Almost everyone knows Nancy and thinks that she's doing a great job. And the girls in the city look at Nancy and say to themselves, "I too can be a police officer or anything else I want to be."

COMPREHENSION QUESTIONS

Answer these questions about the story. *Use your experience and own ideas to answer questions with an asterisk (*). Work in pairs or small groups. The numbers in parentheses tell you which paragraph in the story has the answer.*

1. When the city first hired female police officers, what did many people wonder? (1)
2. What two questions did many people ask? (1)
3. Today, how do most people in the city feel about having women police officers? (2)
*4. Why do think that Dave didn't want to work with Nancy?
5. What happened when he attempted to arrest a drug dealer? (3)
6. What does Nancy have a lot of? What isn't she afraid of? (4)
*7. How much do you think police officers worry about the risks they must take? A lot? A little? Not at all? Explain your answer.
8. What makes it easy for the other police officers to accept Nancy? (5)
9. Why is she a successful police officer? (6)
10. How does she feel about her job? (7)
11. When do her parents relax? (7)
12. What do the girls in the city say to themselves when they look at Nancy? (8)

GUESSING FROM CONTEXT

Guess the meaning of the key words in these sentences. *Use the context of the story to help you. Circle your answers.*

1. "Would women be strong enough and **tough** enough to do the job," they asked.

   a. smart
   b. fast
   c. big
   d. brave

2. Nancy knows that some still prefer male officers, but it doesn't **bother her.**

   a. disturb her
   b. interest her
   c. make her quit
   d. surprise her

3. Nancy **has a lot of courage** and isn't afraid of danger.

   a. is very polite
   b. is very careful
   c. can do what's very difficult
   d. is very friendly

WORD ENTRIES

> **won·der** / wun′dər / *verb:* to be uncertain about something and to want to know about it; to be curious about something: *I **wonder** what happened to my old friend George.* —*noun* **1:** a person or thing that is amazing: *Niagara Falls is one of the **wonders** of the world.* **2:** the feeling of surprise and admiration that comes from seeing the something amazing.
>
> **tough** / tuf / *adjective* **1:** strong and able to do what is difficult: *Boxers and football players have to be **tough**.* **2:** difficult to do: *That was a **tough** test. I'm glad I studied for it.*
>
> **both·er** / both′ər / *verb:* to disturb; to take away one's peace: *It really **bothers** me when the children don't listen.* —*noun:* a person or thing that disturbs one: *I'll watch your daughter while you go to the store. She's no **bother**.*
>
> **at first** / at fûrst / *idiom:* in the beginning: *Our math course was easy **at first**, but now it's difficult.*

COMPLETING SENTENCES

Complete the sentences with these words. *Use each word twice. Where a word has different endings, both forms are given.*

at first	wonder/wondered	bother/bothers	tough

1. I _____ what time it is.

2. Our boss is kind, but she can also be _____.

3. Don't _____ to cook dinner. We'll eat out tonight.

4. The play was dull _____, but it became interesting.

5. Cleaning the garage was _____ work.

6. Craig _____ how much the bicycle cost.

7. The water felt cold _____, but it feels fine now.

8. My little sister _____ me a lot, but I try to be nice to her.

WORD ENTRIES

> **part·ner** / pärt′nər / *noun:* a person who works, lives, or shares an activity with another: *The dance is going to begin. Does everyone have a **partner**?*
>
> **cour·age** / kûr′ij / *noun:* the ability to do what is dangerous or very difficult: *You need **courage** to be a good soldier.*
>
> **risk** / risk / *noun:* danger; the possibility of loss: *There's very little **risk** when you put your money in the bank.* —*verb:* to put something in danger: *Firefighters **risk** their lives to save people.*
>
> **suc·cess** / sək-ses′ / *noun:* the reaching of a goal; an accomplishment: *The party was a big **success**. Everyone had a good time.*
>
> **suc·cess·ful** / sək-ses′fəl / *adjective:* having reached a goal; having accomplished something: *Ernie works hard. That's why he's a **successful** businessman.*

COMPLETING SENTENCES

Complete the sentences with these words. *Use each word twice. Where a word has different endings, both forms are given.*

courage	success/successful	risk/risks	partner/partners

1. My friend had a serious operation. Fortunately, it was a _____.

2. Amanda is a good driver. She doesn't take unnecessary _____.

3. It takes _____ to quit smoking.

4. Fred and Al own and run a restaurant. They're business _____.

5. Too much weight and too little exercise increase the _____ of a heart attack.

6. Tracy is a _____ writer. Her books are very popular.

7. One of the most important things in life is the choice of a marriage _____.

8. It takes a lot of skill and _____ to be an astronaut.

Discuss or think about these questions before completing the story.

1. What are some of the advantages of owning your own business?
2. What are some of the disadvantages?
3. What would a person have to do to open a store?

Complete the story with these words.

courage	success	bothered	tough
risk	partners	at first	wondered

Their Own Business

Brenda and her friend Lucy used to work in a shoe store. They liked their work and they liked Henry, the owner of the store. He was pleasant and easy to work for, but he didn't pay them much. They weren't happy about their pay, and they _____ if they should open their own shoe store. They realized they might make a lot of money, or lose a lot. It would be a big _____.

Brenda was eager to open a new store. _____ Lucy didn't like the idea, but she changed her mind. They told Henry they were going to quit and open their own store. This took _____. Henry listened carefully and wished them well. He wasn't happy, but he tried not to show how much their decision _____ him.

Brenda and Lucy became business _____, and they soon discovered how _____ it is to start your own business. They had to borrow money, fix the store, buy shoes, advertise, keep records, and work long hours. They're going to open their store next week. Brenda, Lucy, and their friends hope their store will be a _____, but they can't be sure.

SHARING INFORMATION

Discuss these questions and topics in pairs or small groups.

1. Complete two of the following sentences. **I wonder** where _____.
   I wonder if _____. **I wonder** how much _____.

2. Name something you did or something you're doing that's **tough** to do.

3. Name some ways in which students **bother** teachers.

4. Complete the following sentences. I started to learn English _____
   ago. **At first** _____.

5. Married couples are **partners**, and love is the most important thing in this
   partnership. But it's not the only important thing. How important is it for
   marriage partners to share common interests—to like to do and talk about the
   same things? Explain your answer.

6. Some say **courage** is to act without fear in a dangerous situation. Others say
   that courage is to do what is dangerous although we're afraid. What do you
   think?

7. We cannot live without taking **risks**. Name some ordinary risks we take with
   little or no worry.

8. Everyone wants to be a **success**. What do you think *you* have to do to be a
   success in life?

WORD FAMILIES

Complete the sentences with these words. *If necessary, add an ending to the word so it
forms a correct sentence.* (adj. = adjective and adv. = adverb)

1. **to wonder** (verb)   **wonderful** (adj.)

   A. That was a great dinner. You're a _____ cook!

   B. I _____ where I left my wallet.

2. **partner** (noun)   **partnership** (noun)

   A. Ralph and I often study together. We're study _____.

   B. Linda and Cathy are forming a _____. They're lawyers.

3. **courage** (noun) **courageous** (adj.) **to encourage** (verb)

   encouragement (noun) **to discourage** (verb) **discouragement** (noun)

   A. Banks _____ people to save money.

   B. Gandhi was a _____ leader who helped India win independence.

   C. High prices _____ people from buying homes.

   D. Jennifer has been sick for two weeks and isn't improving. Her _____ is understandable.

   E. It took _____ to tell the president that he was wrong.

   F. Our team is losing badly. The players need some _____ from their coach and fans.

4. **risk** (noun) **risky** (adj.)

   A. Every time you get in a car, there's a slight _____.

   B. The roads are covered with ice. It's too _____ to drive.

5. **success** (noun) **to succeed** (verb) **unsuccessful** (adj.)

   A. If at first you don't _____, try again.

   B. I tried to run a mile in five minutes, but I was _____.

   C. The concert was a _____. It made money and everyone enjoyed the music.

BUILDING ADJECTIVES WITH -ING

The suffix **-ing** is added to verbs to form an adjective. For example, *excite + ing = exciting; understand + ing = understanding.*

The suffix **-ing** adds no special meaning to the verb.

Verb	Adjective	Verb	Adjective
amaze	amazing	interest	interesting
burn	burning	last	lasting
come	coming	love	loving
die	dying	miss	missing
encourage	encouraging	will	willing
excite	exciting	win	winning
follow	following	understand	understanding

Circle the letter next to the word that best completes the sentence.

1. The election was close and very _____.

   a. understanding   c. loving

   b. exciting   d. lasting

2. They've looked everywhere for the _____ child, but they can't find her.

   a. willing   c. interesting

   b. amazing   d. missing

3. I got some _____ news from my doctor. I'm well enough to leave the hospital.

   a. loving   c. encouraging

   b. lasting   d. winning

4. You have an hour to answer the _____ questions.

   a. following   c. coming

   b. amazing   d. willing

5. Angel spends a lot of time with his children. He's a (an) _____ father.

   a. lasting   c. loving

   b. amazing   d. exciting

6. They're going to cut down the _____ trees and plant new ones.

   a. willing   c. lasting

   b. dying   d. interesting

7. If you have the _____ numbers in this week's lottery, you'll be rich—8, 43, 17.

   a. winning   c. missing

   b. amazing   d. following

8. Mr. Patel always has time to listen to and help his students. He's a (an) _____ teacher.

   a. interesting   c. understanding

   b. winning   d. exciting

USING THE INTERNET TO FIND INFORMATION

1. *Enter* the keywords **female police officers in the United States** *in the search box of any general search engine such as Google or Yahoo. Click on the "search" button or hit "enter" on the keyboard. The search engine will lead you to a list of Web sites.*

   Click on the links to two or three of these Web sites. Look over these sites and choose the one that seems the most interesting and that tells you the most about female police officers. Read a page or two. (Option: write down two or three things you learned about female police officers from this site.)

2. *Enter* the keywords **facts, Pennsylvania** *in the search box of any general search engine such as Google or Yahoo. Click on the "search" button or hit "enter" on the keyboard. The search engine will lead you to a list of Web sites.*

   Click on the links to two or three of these Web sites. Look over these sites and choose the one that seems the most interesting and that tells you the most about Pennsylvania. Read a page or two. (Option: write down two or three things you learned about Pennsylvania from this site.)

SYNONYMS

Next to each sentence, write the word that has the same meaning or almost the same meaning as the part of the sentence in bold print.

tough	reply	rather	approaching
stole	risk	chase	bothers

1. _____ I don't let my son swim alone. There's too much **danger.**

2. _____ We're **getting close to** the bridge.

3. _____ Mrs. Lopez works full-time and has three young children. That's **difficult.**

4. _____ Throw the stick. The dog will **run to get** it and bring it back.

5. _____ Someone **took** Eva's coat.

6. _____ May I have a glass of water, please? I'm **quite** thirsty.

7. _____ Our math teacher won't let us talk in class. It **disturbs** her.

8. _____ Ryan e-mailed his parents to ask for money. He hopes they'll **answer** soon.

SENTENCE COMPLETION

Complete the sentences with these words.

recognize	thieves	applied	partners
threatened	appointment	mild	suggested

1. Mr. Martini is a very good lawyer, but you have to wait three weeks for an _____ to see him.

2. Pam _____ that we go to the beach tomorrow. What do you think?

3. The teacher _____ to give her a zero for cheating on a test.

4. Lisa and her cousin are business _____. They run the gift shop on the corner.

5. Car _____ are good at getting into locked cars.

6. We had a _____ winter—only three inches of snow.

7. Do you _____ the woman in the red dress?

8. I _____ for a loan yesterday. I hope I get it.

STORY COMPLETION

Complete the story with these words.

aware	therefore	reach	wondered
success	at first	courage	eager

Christopher Columbus

Christopher Columbus is probably the world's most famous explorer. He believed the world was round, and he was _____ to find a new and shorter way to _____ the Indies. He planned to do this by sailing west from Europe. No one had ever tried this before.

_____ Columbus couldn't get the money he needed for the trip. He asked the King of Portugal for help, but he said no. Finally, Queen Isabella of Spain gave him the money.

In 1492, Columbus and his men sailed from Spain in three ships, the Niña, the Pinta, and the Santa Maria. They were _____ of the problems and dangers of trying to cross the ocean in three small ships, but they were men of great _____.

They sailed for weeks without seeing land. The sailors began to lose hope and _____ if they would ever see land again. They wanted to go back to Spain, but Columbus got them to continue.

Then on October 12, 1492, one of the sailors saw a small island; this made them very happy. They landed on the island, and Columbus named it San Salvador. Their trip was a _____.

Columbus thought that the island was part of the Indies. _____, he called the Native Americans he met there Indians.

WORD LIST

The key words are listed in alphabetical order. The words derived from them are indented and immediately follow the key words. The derived words are not in alphabetical order.

drag 80
dream 115
dull 89

E

eager 175
   eagerly 179
   eagerness 179
earn 89
   earnings 92
edge 70
enjoy 22
   enjoyment 24
   enjoyable 24
enough 115
exciting 141
   excite 144
   excitement 144
expensive 55
   expense 58
explore 45
   explorer 49
   exploration 49

F

fall asleep 125
   asleep 128
fan 141
far 5
fault 152
fool 90
foolish 90
   foolishly 92
   foolishness 92
fortunately 45
   fortunate 49
   unfortunate 49
   unfortunately 49
fun 36
   funny 39

H

hardly 125
hate 36
   hatred 39
have to 5
hesitate 79
   hesitant 83
   hesitantly 83
   hesitation 83
however 14
huge 80
hunt 79
hunter 79
   hunting 83
hurry 6

I

instead 162
   instead of 162
improve 36
   improvement 39

J

join 142
just 56

L

lift 80
loan 56
lose 21
   loser 24
   loss 24
   lost 24

M

main 161
   mainly 165
may 14
mild 185
   mildly 181

miss 5
   missing 8
mistake 45
   mistaken 49

N

neighbor 55
   neighborhood 58

O

of course 55
only 21
own 13
   owner 16

P

pain 162
   painful 165
   painless 165
partner 196
   partnership 198
pinch 126
poison 46
   poisonous 49
pool 69
prefer 69
   preference 72
   preferable 72
protect 13
   protection 16
   protective 16
   protector 16
proud (of) 45
   proudly 49
   pride 49

Q

quick 6
   quickly 8
quit 89
quite 106

LIST OF KEY WORDS

Chapter 1
1. far
2. miss
3. too
4. have to
5. hurry
6. waste
7. quick
8. around

Chapter 2
1. a lot of
   a lot
2. afraid
3. own
4. protect
5. however
6. bite
7. trust
8. may

Chapter 3
1. only
2. weigh
   weight
3. lose
4. although
5. try
6. almost
7. starve
8. enjoy

Chapter 4
1. both
2. share
3. burn
4. still
5. improve
6. fun
7. wipe
8. hate

Chapter 5
1. proud
2. explore
3. fortunately
4. mistake
5. swallow
6. poison
7. rush
8. bit

Chapter 6
1. of course
2. expensive
3. neighbor
4. afford
5. choose
6. just
7. loan
8. borrow

Chapter 7
1. spend
2. average
3. prefer
4. pool
5. dive
6. deep
7. shallow
8. edge

Chapter 8
1. hunt
   hunter
2. shoot
3. stream
4. hesitate
5. aim
6. huge
7. lift
8. drag

Chapter 9
1. quit
2. at least
3. dull
4. earn
5. fool
   foolish
6. argue
   argument
7. shout
8. bitter

Chapter 10
1. ago
2. struggle
3. be used to
4. storm
5. skill
6. bake
   baker
   bakery
7. accomplish
8. quite

Chapter 11
1. enough
2. dream
3. search
4. crack
5. repair
6. advantage
7. so
8. require

Chapter 12
1. weary
2. fall asleep
3. hardly
4. while
5. pinch
6. wake up
7. shame
   ashamed
8. disturb

Chapter 13
1. fan
2. amaze
3. discover
4. exciting
5. join
6. crowd
7. cheer
8. score

Chapter 14
1. attempt
2. cautious
3. suddenly
4. crash
5. damage
6. slight
7. fault
8. blame

Chapter 15
1. main
2. warn
   warning
3. used to
4. dangerous
5. pain
6. worry
7. right away
8. instead
   instead of

Chapter 16
1. therefore
2. appointment
3. apply
4. eager
5. rather
6. suggest
7. reply
8. aware

Chapter 17
1. mild
2. approach
3. thief
4. threaten
5. steal
6. chase
7. reach
8. recognize

Chapter 18
1. wonder
2. tough
3. bother
4. at first
5. partner
6. courage
7. risk
8. success
   successful